# Impact English

MIKE GOULD, KIM RICHARDSON, MARY GREEN & JOHN MANNION

**Key Stage 3 – Year 7 • Student Book 1**

# Contents

## Unit 5 Drama in the making



## Unit 6 Far from home



## Unit 7 Media today



## Unit 8 Past lives



## Unit 9 Sporting challenge

# Unit 1 Terror in the night

## 1 A horror story

Aims

- Read a short story
- Learn how to scan a text (R2)
- Learn about story endings (Wr5)

---

**This story comes from *More Horowitz Horror* by Anthony Horowitz. When you come to the end, *don't do what the story asks you to do – yet*! You will follow this up later.**

### THE SHORTEST HORROR STORY EVER WRITTEN

I want to tell you how this story got included in this book.
About a week before the book was published, I broke into the offices of Orchard Books which are located in a rather grubby street near Liverpool Street Station. Maybe you haven't noticed but the
5 book you are holding at this very minute was published by Orchard and I wanted to get my hands on it because, you see, I'd had an idea.
Generally speaking, publishers are stupid lazy people. Orchard Books have about twenty people working for them but not one of them noticed that a window had been forced open in the middle of
10 the night and that someone had added a couple of pages to the collection of horror stories that was sitting by the computer, waiting to be sent to the printers. I had brought these pages with me, you see, because I wanted to add my own message to the book. Nobody noticed and nobody cared

15 and if you are reading this then I'm afraid my plan has worked and you are about to discover the meaning of true horror. Get ready – because here it comes.

Twelve years ago I desperately wanted to be a writer and so I wrote a horror story (based on my own experiences) which was rejected by 20 every publisher in London because, they claimed, it wasn't frightening enough! Of course, none of them had the faintest idea what horror really meant because they had never actually committed a murder whereas I, my dear reader, had committed several.

My Uncle Frederick was my first victim, followed by my next-door 25 neighbour (an unpleasant little man with a moustache and a smelly cat), two total strangers, an actor who once had a bit part in EastEnders and a Jehovah's Witness who happened to knock at my door while I was cooking lunch. Unfortunately my adventures came to an end when a dim-witted policeman stopped my car just as I was 30 disposing of the last body and I was arrested and sent to a lunatic asylum for life. Recently, however, I escaped and it was after that that I had the wonderful idea which you are reading about at this very moment and which can be summarised in three simple stages. Drop into the offices of one of those smarmy publishers in London and slip 35 a couple of pages into somebody else's book (with many apologies to Anthony Horowitz, whoever he may be). Exit quietly and stay in hiding until the book is published. Return only when the book is in the shops and then wait in the background, until some poor fool buys it and follow that person home…

40 Yes, dear reader, at this very moment I could be sitting outside your home or your school or wherever you happen to be and if by any chance you are the one I've chosen, I'm afraid you're about to learn a lesson about horror that I know you'd prefer to miss. Orchard Books 45 are also going to wish they had published me all those years ago, especially when they start losing readers in particularly nasty ways, one by one. Understanding will come – but I'm afraid you're going to have to read this story all over again.

50 Start at the beginning. Only this time look carefully at the first word of each sentence. Or to be more precise, the first letter of each first word. Now, at last, I hope you can see quite how gloriously, hideously mad I really am – although for you, perhaps, it may already be too late.

**Jehovah's Witness** a Christian group that believes the end of the world is near

## Key Reading

### Narrative texts

The text is a story or **narrative**. The purpose of a narrative is to entertain us.

The main feature of a narrative text is:

- It has a structure that includes an opening (**introduction**), a problem (**complication**), a dramatic moment when everything comes to a head (**crisis**) and an ending (**resolution**) when things are sorted out.

*The Shortest Horror Story Ever Written* follows this structure – up to a point!

- **Introduction**: We find out how the story got into the book.
- **Complication**: The 'writer' is a murderer seeking revenge.

**1** Now **discuss whether or not you agree** with these statements.
**a)** The crisis has not happened yet.
**b)** The story has no ending.

**2** The writer tells us that he slips his story into someone else's book, and says, '(with many apologies to Anthony Horowitz, whoever he may be)'.
**Who** do you think really wrote the story?

## Purpose

**3** **Why** do you think he really wrote this story? You can choose more than one reason.

- To scare the reader.
- To make the reader laugh.
- The writer is mad.
- The writer wants to enjoy himself.

**4** What is the **main reason** from the answers you chose in question 3? Discuss your ideas.

## Reading for meaning

Now you are going to work out the hidden message in the story. To do this you will need to find key letters and write them down. This means you will **scan** the text.

**Scanning** a text is a good way to get information quickly. It means you skip words to find what you are looking for.

- Start by finding the first word of every sentence in the story.
- Then, find the first letter of each word, like this:

> **I** want to tell you how this story got included in this book.
>
> **A**bout a week before the book was published, I broke into the offices of Orchard Books which are located in a rather grubby street near Liverpool Street Station. **M**aybe you haven't noticed...

- So the message begins: **I am**.

R2 **5** Find all the **first letters** from the first word in each sentence, write them down and read the message.

**6** **Scan the text** to find:
**a)** the station near Orchard Books (paragraph 2)
**b)** the name of the writer's uncle (paragraph 5)
**c)** the person who caught the writer (paragraph 5)
**d)** where the writer could be waiting for the reader (paragraph 6).

## Focus on: Story endings

*The Shortest Horror Story Ever Written* has a twist or surprise at the end.

**7** What is the **twist** in the picture story below?

The End　　　　Not quite...

As you see, a story with a twist can mean that the story has not ended.

This is also true of **cliffhangers**. These often come at the end of a chapter in a book. They create tension or **suspense**. For example:

All at once there was a clattering of hooves. A ghost-rider appeared. He grasped a flaming torch in his hand. Then another came and another and another. They swung the torches above their heads. They hurled them into the crowd. As the people fled, a noise like the sound of thunder came from behind the hill. Slowly, a giant shadow loomed and then something appeared. Something more dreadful than anything the people had seen before.

In writing like this, it is a good idea to vary the sentences. This makes the writing more interesting. It keeps the reader's attention.

He grasped a flaming torch in his hand.

We could change this sentence around:

In his hand he grasped a flaming torch.

**8** Change the first of these sentences around.

They swung the torches above their heads. They hurled them into the crowd.

Read the two sentences together. They should sound better.

## Key Writing

Wr5, S11

**9** Read this extract and **finish the last sentence**. Then **write another 100 words** to build up the tension and end with a cliffhanger. Remember to vary your sentences.

I pushed open the great oak door. It creaked. I stopped and listened. There were no voices. I slipped out and walked straight towards the iron gates. I could hear my feet crunching on the gravel. Eight, nine, ten, I was almost there. Then suddenly the ground underneath me began to shake and from its depths came…

#  Big fears

## Aims

- Read the poem, *Big Fears*
- Learn what 'writing in lines' means (R14)
- Learn how punctuation is used
- Learn what 'repetition' means
- Write a poem (Wr8)

---

**We all have our own fears and worries. At night they seem to grow. Read this poem by John Rice and find out what Sian, Matthew and Karen worry about.**

### Big Fears

Twenty-five feet above Sian's house
hangs a thick wire cable
that droops and sags between two
electricity pylons.
5 A notice says it carries 40,000 volts
from one metallic scarecrow to the next,
then on to the next and the next
right across the countryside to the city.
The cable sways above Sian's council house
10 making her radio crackle and sometimes
making her television go on the blink.

If it's a very windy night
Sian gets frightened because she
thinks the cable might snap,
15 fall onto the roof and electrocute
everyone as they sleep.

This is Sian's Big Fear.

Outside Matthew's bedroom there
is a tall tree. Taller than the house.
20 In summer it is heavy with huge leaves.
In winter it stands lonely as a morning moon.

On a windy night, Matthew worries
that the tree might be blown down
and crash through his bedroom window.
25 It would certainly kill him and his cat
if it wasn't in its own cardboard box.

This is Matthew's Big Fear.

Outside Karen's bedroom there's nothing
but a pleasant view, meadows, hedges, sheep
30 and some distant gentle hills.
There's nothing sinister, nothing to worry about.

But in the dark Karen thinks
the darting shapes on the ceiling
are really the shadows of a ghost's
35 great cold hands and that the night noises
made by the water pipes are the
screeches and groans of attic skeletons.

**(to) electrocute** to be hurt or killed by electric shock

**pylons** huge metal structures that carry electricity cables

**volts** units of electric current or force

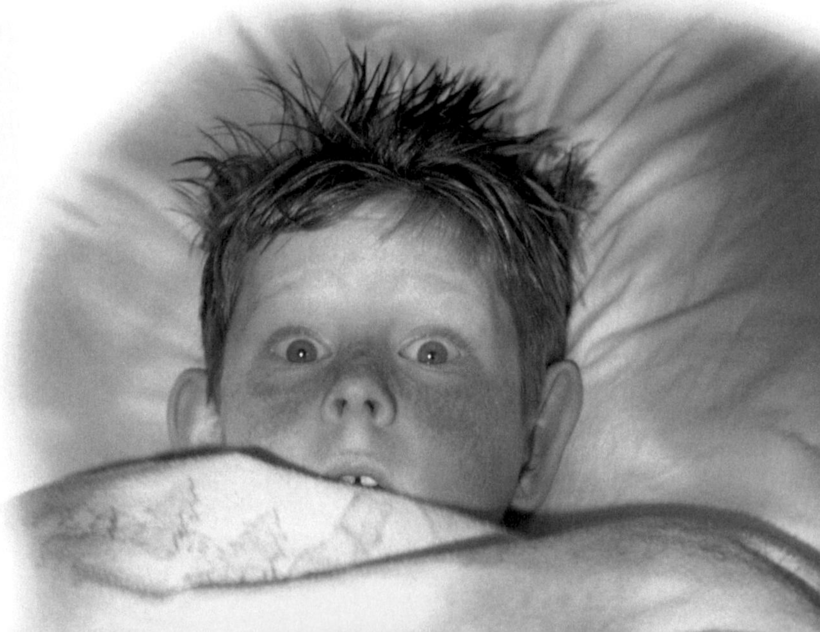

# Key Reading

## Poetry

This text is a poem. Its **purpose** is to explore feelings and ideas.

A poem is made up of **images**, **rhythm** and **form**.

- The **images** are the pictures made by the words.
- The **rhythm** is like the beat in music.
- The **form** is the framework or pattern of the poem. Poems are written in **lines** not sentences.

Poems can be written in different styles:

- Some poems **rhyme**. For example, doom/gloom/tomb.
- Some poems are **free verse**. They have lines of different lengths with different rhythms. (Some free verse contains rhyme.)

To work out the rhythm of *Big Fears*, listen to those parts of words (**syllables**) that are stressed. For example, '*twen-ty*' has two syllables. We stress the syllable '*twen-*'; the other syllable ('*-ty*') is unstressed.

**1** **a)** Gently **tap out the rhythm** of this line from *Big Fears*.

> Twenty-five feet above Sian's house
> hangs a thick wire cable
> that droops and sags between two
> electricity pylons.

**b)** Do the lines have the **same rhythm**?

**2** Are the lines the **same length**?

**3** Below are four statements about the poem. Which of them are **true**?

**a)** It has the same rhythm in each line.
**b)** It has lines of the same length.
**c)** It is a free verse poem.

## Purpose

*Big Fears* explores different feelings and ideas about fear. Sometimes fears are based on real things or things that could happen.

**4** Which fears in the poem are based on **real** things?

## Reading for meaning

When writing in lines, words that are used in sentences are sometimes dropped. This can add to the impact of a poem.

Outside Matthew's bedroom there is a tall tree. Taller than the house.

If this line was written as sentences, it would read:

Outside Matthew's bedroom there is a tall tree. *It is* taller than the house.

Without 'It is', the words, '...tall tree. Taller...' are closer together. This stresses the height of the tree.

The lines also read differently – the reader's voice rises and falls more in the lines than in the sentences. For example, more stress is put on the word 'Taller' in the lines. Again, this draws attention to the height of the tree.

R14

**5** **Read the two lines** and the two full sentences again, listening to the difference in your voice.

**6** **a)** Now read this sentence:

At night when I hear the tap, tap, tap of the branch on the window I dream of ghosts.

To create a poem you could write out the sentence in lines. It could begin.

At night I hear the
tap,
tap,
tap,

**b) Finish writing the sentence** above in lines:

- Choose where to begin and end them.
- Think about the sound of the branch.

**7** Read your lines and **listen to your voice** rising and falling.

## Focus on: Punctuation and repetition

**Punctuation** can add to the meaning of a poem.

no comma, read on

> Outside Karen's bedroom there's nothing
> but a pleasant view, meadows, hedges, sheep
> and some distant gentle hills.
> There's nothing sinister, nothing to worry about.

full stop, longer pause

comma, slight pause

The first three lines work together. The last line is a comment on what is outside Karen's bedroom.

**8** **a) Read the verse again**. As you do, read the last line as though you are trying to convince yourself there is 'nothing to worry about'.
**b**) Now **read the last line** as though there *is* something to worry about!
**c)** How else could you read the last line? Try **changing your voice** to suit different meanings.

**Repetition** in a poem means there are repeating words or lines. This helps to give the poem a pattern or framework (**form**). It also helps to emphasise what the poem is about, as shown in this verse from *Big Fears*.

If it's a very windy night
Sian gets frightened because she
thinks the cable might snap,
fall onto the roof and electrocute
everyone as they sleep.

This is Sian's Big Fear.

This line is repeated in the poem

**9** **a)** What else in the last line tells us that the poem is about **fear**?
**b)** Why do you think this line is **set apart** from the other lines?
**c)** Where else does the **repeating line** occur in the poem?
**d)** The line could be written in **another place** in the poem. Where would that be? Why?

## Key Writing

**10** **a)** Refer back to the lines you wrote in question 6.

**b)** Choose the lines you like best as the start of a **short free verse poem** about ghosts. In your poem, include:

- a ghostly event
- different sentence lengths
- varied line breaks
- punctuation to help read the poem
- a repeating line about ghosts.

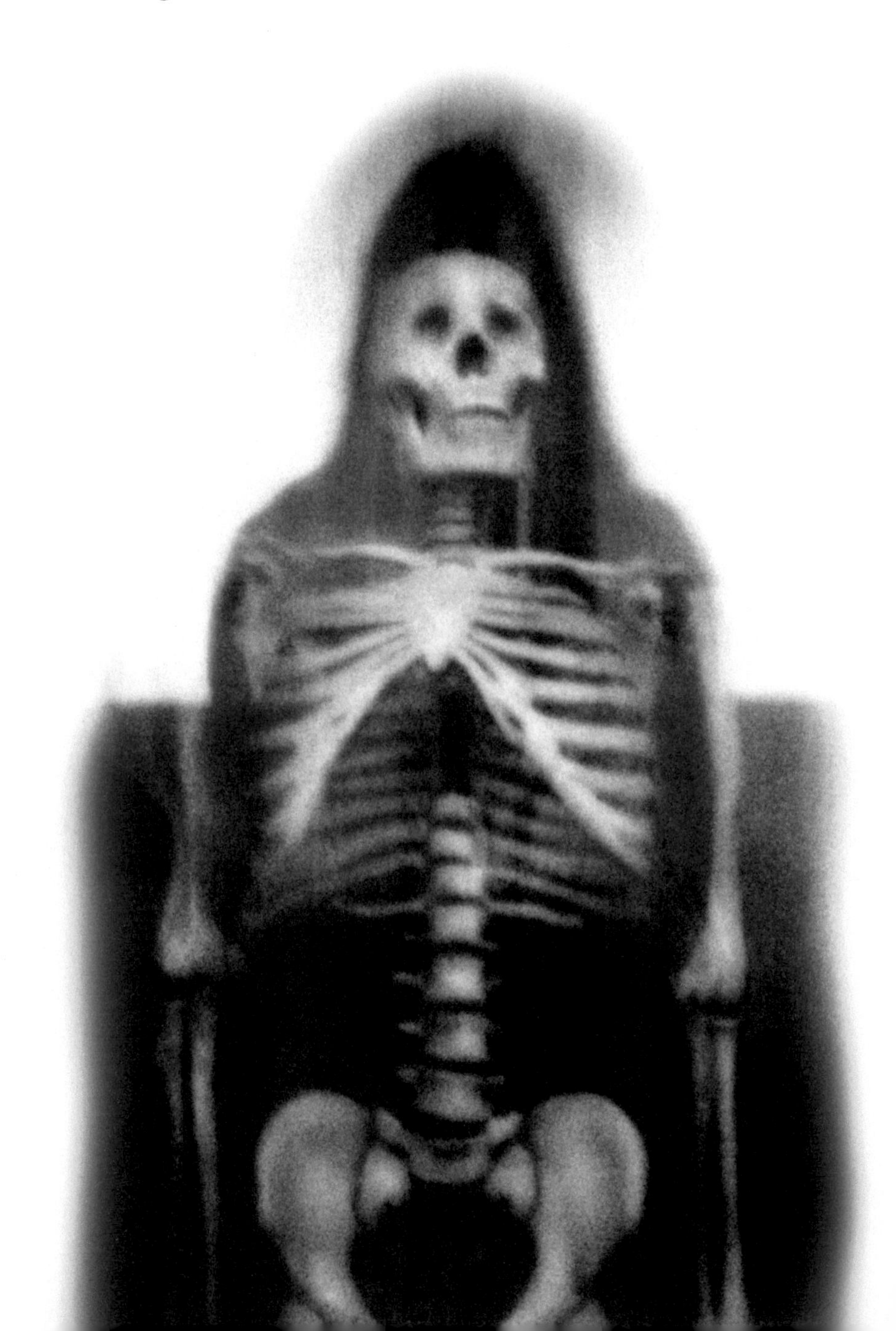

# 3 All in the mind

## Aims

- Read an argument text
- Use paragraphs to follow the main points (R7)
- Record points in a flow chart (Wr2)
- Consider other points of view and express your own (S&L11)

**Do ghosts really exist? Read the following article from a BBC webpage and find out!**

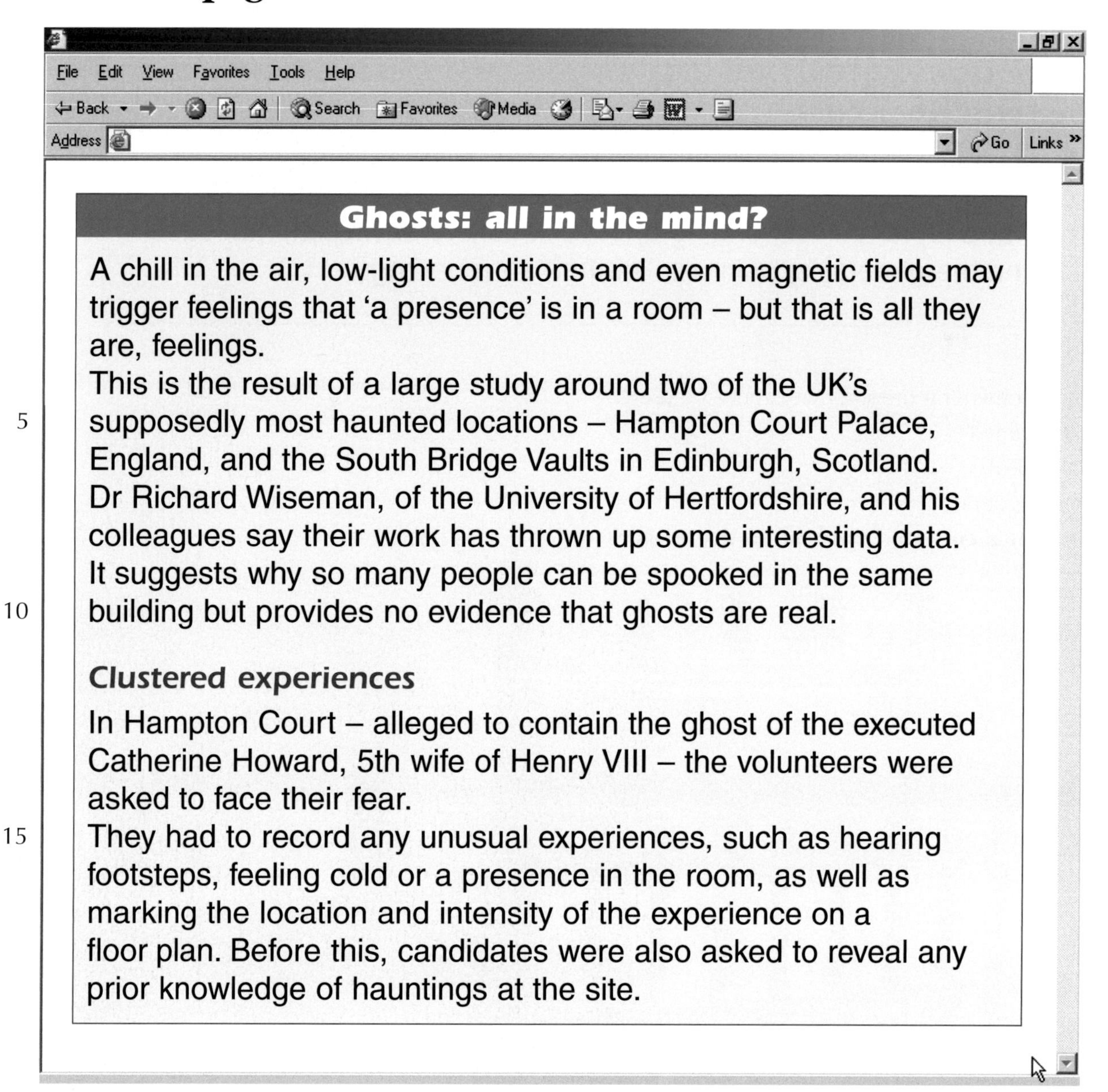


### Ghosts: all in the mind?

A chill in the air, low-light conditions and even magnetic fields may trigger feelings that 'a presence' is in a room – but that is all they are, feelings.

This is the result of a large study around two of the UK's supposedly most haunted locations – Hampton Court Palace, England, and the South Bridge Vaults in Edinburgh, Scotland.

Dr Richard Wiseman, of the University of Hertfordshire, and his colleagues say their work has thrown up some interesting data.

It suggests why so many people can be spooked in the same building but provides no evidence that ghosts are real.

#### Clustered experiences

In Hampton Court – alleged to contain the ghost of the executed Catherine Howard, 5th wife of Henry VIII – the volunteers were asked to face their fear.

They had to record any unusual experiences, such as hearing footsteps, feeling cold or a presence in the room, as well as marking the location and intensity of the experience on a floor plan. Before this, candidates were also asked to reveal any prior knowledge of hauntings at the site.

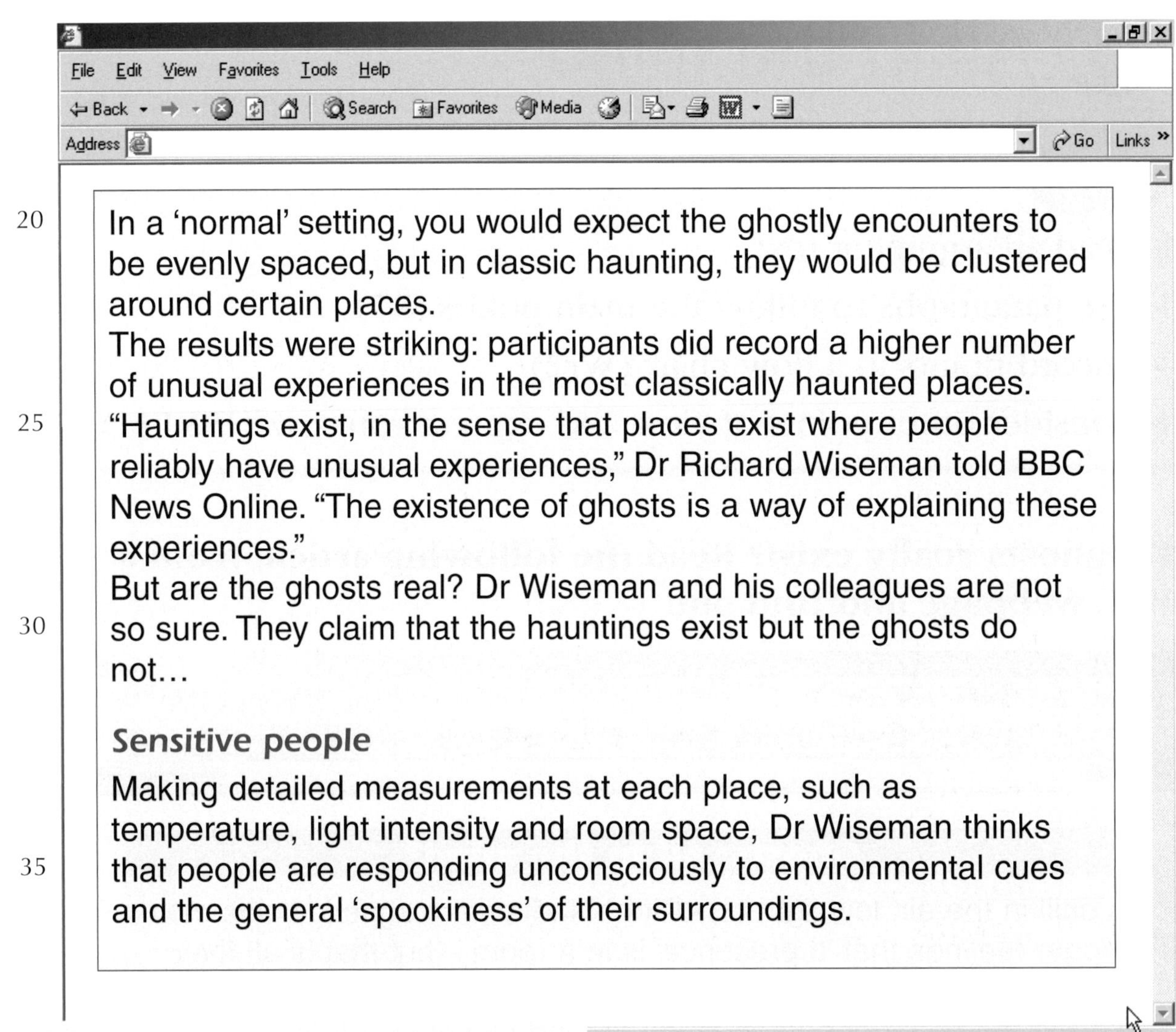


20 In a 'normal' setting, you would expect the ghostly encounters to be evenly spaced, but in classic haunting, they would be clustered around certain places.
The results were striking: participants did record a higher number of unusual experiences in the most classically haunted places.
25 "Hauntings exist, in the sense that places exist where people reliably have unusual experiences," Dr Richard Wiseman told BBC News Online. "The existence of ghosts is a way of explaining these experiences."
But are the ghosts real? Dr Wiseman and his colleagues are not
30 so sure. They claim that the hauntings exist but the ghosts do not…

## Sensitive people

Making detailed measurements at each place, such as temperature, light intensity and room space, Dr Wiseman thinks
35 that people are responding unconsciously to environmental cues and the general 'spookiness' of their surroundings.

**presence** something present that cannot be seen
**alleged** claimed
**classic** typical
**clustered** grouped together
**environmental cues** things around us that trigger certain thoughts

## Key Reading

### Argument texts

This text is a report that contains an **argument**. The **purpose** of an argument is to present a **point of view** so that others will accept it.

The main features of an argument text are:

- It presents an argument clearly, making **points** one at a time.
- It uses **evidence** to back up points. For example, 'Dr Richard Wiseman…and his colleagues…say…'
- It uses **connectives** that help link one idea with another. For example, 'It suggests why…*but*…'
- It is mainly told in the **present tense**. For example, '…that *is* all they are…'
- It may use other tenses. For example, 'They *had* to record …' (past tense).

**1** In paragraph 2, find an example of the **present tense**. What is it referring to?

**2** a) **What tense** is the verb in the following sentence?

The volunteers *were asked* to face their fear.

b) **Why** is it written in this tense?

**3** **Find the verb** in the first sentence that tells us something *might* happen.

## Purpose

**4** Is the purpose of this argument to show that:
**a)** ghosts exist
**b)** ghosts do not exist?

## Reading for meaning

In order to follow an argument, you need to understand:

- the **topic** of the argument
- the **main points** being made
- the **evidence** given for these points.

The opening section of the article gives the reader an idea of what the text is about. It answers some basic **questions**, such as:

- What?
- Where?
- Who?

**5** Look at the two questions in the chart below. Find the places in the text where the questions are **answered**.

| Question | Answer |
|---|---|
| What is the argument? | Ghosts do not exist, but there are places where people feel 'haunted'. |
| What is the evidence? | The results of a large study. |

**6** **a)** Look over the article again and **write two questions** of your own:
- Question 1 should begin with **where...?**
- Question 2 should begin with **who...?**

**b)** Ask a partner to answer your questions.

### The main points of an argument

The text can also help us to find the main points of an argument.

- Sub-headings help us to find information.
- The first few words of a paragraph can give us clues.

Look at the following examples from the text.

**Sub-heading:** 'Clustered experiences'

**First few words of paragraphs:**

- 'In Hampton Court…'
- 'They had to record…'
- 'The results were striking…'

From this information, you can tell what these paragraphs are about.

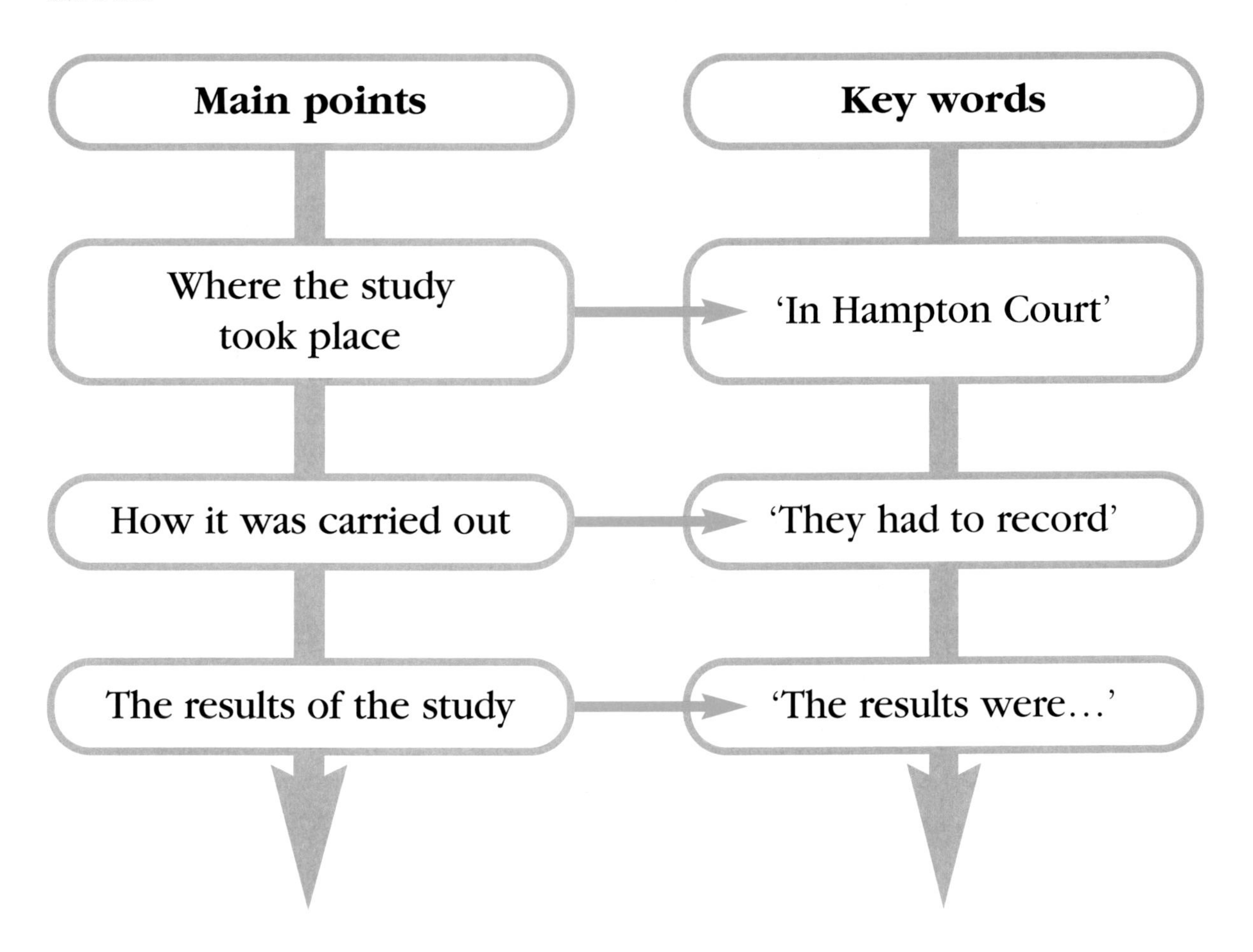

**7** **a)** Find the **first words** of the last three paragraphs of the article.
**b)** Decide what the **main points** are.
**c)** Sketch out the **flow chart** on page 23. Add your new points to complete it.

## Focus on: Presenting the evidence

Evidence is given to back up the main argument in the text: that ghosts do not exist. It is taken from Dr Wiseman's study.

**8** **Scan the text** to find all the places where Dr Wiseman is mentioned.

**9** In which part of the text is most of the **evidence** given:
- the beginning
- the middle
- the end?

**10** **a)** What 'detailed measurements' did Dr Wiseman and his colleagues make? **Find the words** that tell you.
**b)** Now finish these sentences:
- Dr Wiseman and his colleagues claim…
- Their results show that in haunted places, people…

## Key Speaking and Listening

**11** **a)** In a group, **discuss** the following issue: 'Do you believe in ghosts?'
- Focus on the **evidence** you have studied. Put forward your point of view. Discuss:
  – what the scientists say
  – what the results were and what they meant.
- Use some of your own words and some of the words you have learned. For example, 'Scientists claim…', 'Results show…'.

**b)** Choose someone from your group to **report back** to the class.

# 4 Unit 1 Assignment: The poet

## Assessment Focuses

- AF1 Write imaginative, interesting and thoughtful texts

**You:** are a poet.
**Your task:** to write a poem about horror.

## Stage 1

Most feelings can be compared to something concrete. For example, jealousy is sometimes called 'the green-eyed monster'.

Some other things to compare horror with are:

- the red-eyed monster
- the sudden fever
- the icy chill.

**Add more descriptions** to the list.
Use a thesaurus to help you.
It may help to think of some scary situations.

## Stage 2

A **simile** compares one thing with another using **like** or **as**.

Horror is *like* the red-eyed monster.
*As* horrific *as* the red-eyed monster.

A **metaphor** is created when you say one thing **is** something else.

Horror *is* the red-eyed monster.

Using your ideas from Stage 1, **create similes and metaphors**. Then try to develop lines for your poem. For example, start with a metaphor and add a simile:

metaphor

The red-eyed monster is like a shadow.

simile

Then replace the verb with a new one ending '-ing':

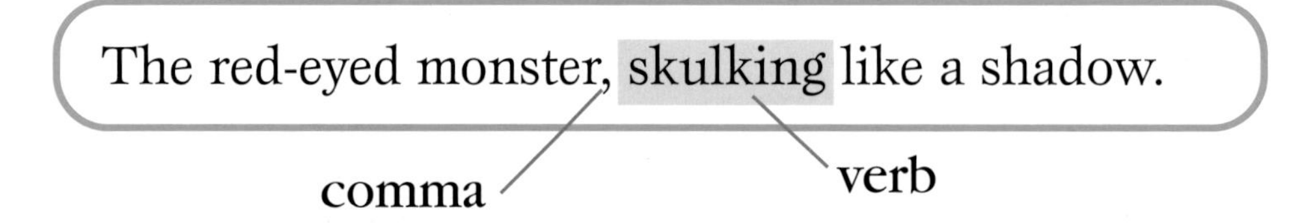


Find interesting verbs in a thesaurus.

## Stage 3

Use the work you have done to **write a free verse poem** about horror. You will need to think about the **form** of your poem.

You could repeat starter words, for example,

'Horror is...:
The red-eyed monster, skulking like a shadow...
The sudden fever...
The...'

Or, you could imagine yourself as 'horror':

'I am the red-eyed monster, skulking like a shadow...
I am...'

Remember to:

- try out different line breaks for emphasis
- choose the version you like best
- think about different ways to end your poem.

### Challenge

Similes and metaphors make **images** (pictures in the mind). The most common images appeal to the sense of sight. But they can also appeal to the other senses: hearing, touch, taste and smell. For example, 'Horror is a fire, seething like a scald/scorch' (touch)

- Write another line to appeal to touch.
- Then write lines for the other senses. Use a thesaurus to find suitable words.
- Add the best lines to your poem.

# Unit 2 Myths and legends

## 1 The apples of the Hesperides

### Aims

- Read a Greek myth
- Think about the purpose of myths and why they have remained popular (R20)
- Discover how a storyteller builds up a picture of the characters (R16)
- Learn why writers vary the length and structure of their sentences, and practise doing this yourself (S18)

---

**This story comes from a book of Ancient Greek myths, retold by Geraldine McCaughrean. The Greek hero Heracles has superhuman strength. But he is the slave of the spiteful King Eurystheus. Before he can be free, he has to complete twelve difficult and dangerous tasks for the king.**

### The Apples of the Hesperides

The twelfth and last of the king's commands was for Heracles to bring him the apples of the Hesperides. These magical fruit grew on a tree in a garden at the end of the world, and around that tree coiled a dragon which never slept.

5 Even Heracles, with all his courage and strength, quailed at the thought of fighting the dragon. So he went to see a giant named Atlas.

Now Atlas was no ordinary giant, as big as a house. Atlas was the biggest man in the world, and towered above houses,

10 trees, cliffs and hills. He was so tall that the gods had given him the task of holding up the sky and keeping the stars from falling. The sun scorched his neck and the new moon shaved his beard. And for thousands of years he had stood in the one spot.

15 "How can I go to the end of the world?" said Atlas, when Heracles asked him for the favour. "How can I go *anywhere*?"

"I could hold the sky for you while you were gone," suggested Heracles.

20 "Could you? Would you? Then I'll do it!" said Atlas.

So Heracles took the sky on his back – though it was the heaviest burden he had ever carried. Atlas stretched himself, then strode away towards the end of the world.

Fetching the apples was no hardship. But as the giant hurried back across the world, carrying the precious fruit, the

25 thought of carrying that weight of sky again seemed less and less attractive. His steps slowed. When at last he reached Heracles – poor, exhausted, bone-bent Heracles – Atlas exclaimed, "I've decided! I'm going to let *you* go on holding up the sky, and *I'll* deliver these apples to King Eurystheus."

30 There was a silence. Then Heracles grunted, "Fine. Thank you. It's a great honour to be allowed to hold up heaven. But if you could just help me get a pad across my shoulders before you go…these stars do prickle…"

35 So Atlas took charge of the sky again – just while Heracles made a pad for his shoulders. He even gave Heracles the apples to hold, because he needed both hands.

"Well, I'll be on my way now," said Heracles, juggling with the apples as he scurried away.

**quailed** trembled, shrank back
**scorched** burnt
**burden** load, weight
**scurried** rushed, scampered

## Key Reading

### Narrative Texts

This text is a **narrative**. Its **purpose** is to tell a story.

The main features of a narrative text are:

- A structure that includes an opening (**introduction**), a problem (**complication**), a dramatic moment when everything comes to a head (**crisis**) and an ending (**resolution**) when things are sorted out. For example, in *The Apples of the Hesperides*, the introduction describes the twelfth task given to Heracles.
- **Characters** who the story is about. The reader often hears their words and thoughts.
- There is also a **narrator**, who tells the story. For example, 'Now Atlas was no ordinary giant', is the narrator telling us about the character Atlas.
- The use of **powerful words**. The narrative must be interesting to read or listen to. For example, 'poor, exhausted, bone-bent Heracles'.

**1** **Draw a cartoon version** of the story. You only have four boxes to fill. What scene will be

**a)** your introduction

**b)** your complication

**c)** your crisis

**d)** your resolution?

**2** Look at paragraph 8 (starting line 23). Which bits tell you what **Atlas says**? Which bits tell you what the **narrator says** about the characters? How do you know?

**3** In the final line the narrator says that Heracles 'scurried away'. Do you think this is better than 'ran away'? Why?

## Purpose

**This narrative entertains us by telling a good story. Myths make good stories for several reasons:**

- **They are often action-packed.**
- **The characters are larger than life, such as gods, heroes and monsters.**

R20

**4** Discuss in pairs what **features** of *The Apples of the Hesperides* make it an entertaining myth. Think about the characters as well as the story.

**5** Myths have another purpose. They say important things about the world and the people in it. In *The Apples of the Hesperides,* Heracles has to complete a really difficult and dangerous task.

**a)** What **qualities** does he show in the way he manages to complete the task?

**b)** Think of a **difficult task** that you managed to complete. What qualities did you show?

## Reading for meaning

**6** There are four characters in *The Apples of the Hesperides.* These are: Heracles, Atlas, King Eurystheus and the dragon. Who are the two main characters in the story?

A storyteller builds up a picture of the characters in three main ways:

- **By describing what they do.**
  This is a description of Atlas: 'For thousands of years he had stood in the one spot.' The description shows us how strong and patient Atlas must be.
- **By telling us what they say.**
  This is what Atlas says when Heracles asks him to get the apples: 'How can I go *anywhere*?' Atlas's words show how puzzled and annoyed he must be.
- **By telling us how they look or feel.**
  This is how the narrator describes Heracles: 'poor, exhausted, bone-bent Heracles'. These three adjectives show us how much Heracles has been suffering under the weight of the sky.

R16

**7** Now write down answers to these questions about paragraph 2:

**a)** How does the narrator **describe** Heracles?
**b)** What does the narrator say that Heracles **felt**?
**c)** What does the narrator say that Heracles **does**?

**8** Find:

**a)** One example of what Atlas **does** (paragraphs 3 or 8)
**b)** One example of what he **says** (paragraphs 4, 6 or 8)
**c)** One example of how he **looks or feels** (paragraph 8).

**Discuss** how each example builds up a picture of the character of Atlas for the reader.

## Focus on: Sentence structure

Good storytellers vary the length of their sentences to keep the reader interested. Look at this example:

A short, clear sentence to start the paragraph

Fetching the apples was no hardship. But as the giant hurried back across the world, carrying the precious fruit, the thought of carrying that weight of sky again seemed less and less attractive. His steps slowed.

The second sentence contrasts with the first. It is made up of three separate clauses. The length of the sentence may suggest the long journey that Atlas made

The third sentence is only three words. It suggests Atlas slowing down after the hurry of the sentence before

S18

**9** Look at the second sentence in the example.

**a)** What **three things** are being said about Atlas in the three different clauses?

**b)** Find another sentence in the story with **more than one clause**.

**Grammar for reading**

A **clause** is a part of a sentence. Every clause includes a verb. Some sentences are just one clause, for example: '*Fetching the apples was no hardship.*' Many sentences have two or more clauses, for example: '*The sun scorched his neck* and *the new moon shaved his beard.*' These two clauses are joined by the connective 'and'.

## Key Writing

**10** Change this sentence to make two shorter sentences.

'Heracles wore a lion skin, which he had taken off a fierce lion that he had killed.'

Remember that each sentence must make sense on its own.

**11** Now write a short paragraph describing the moment when Atlas takes the apples from the tree where the dragon waits. Vary the length of your sentences to make your description more interesting and dramatic. You could start like this:

'Atlas saw the fire coming from the dragon's mouth. It was...'

# The science of Superman

- Read a text explaining why Superman is so strong
- Look at how explanation texts are written and organised (S13c, W14)
- Learn about the links between cause and effect, and how they are highlighted
- Write your own short explanation (Wr12)

**The following text comes from a BBC webpage.**

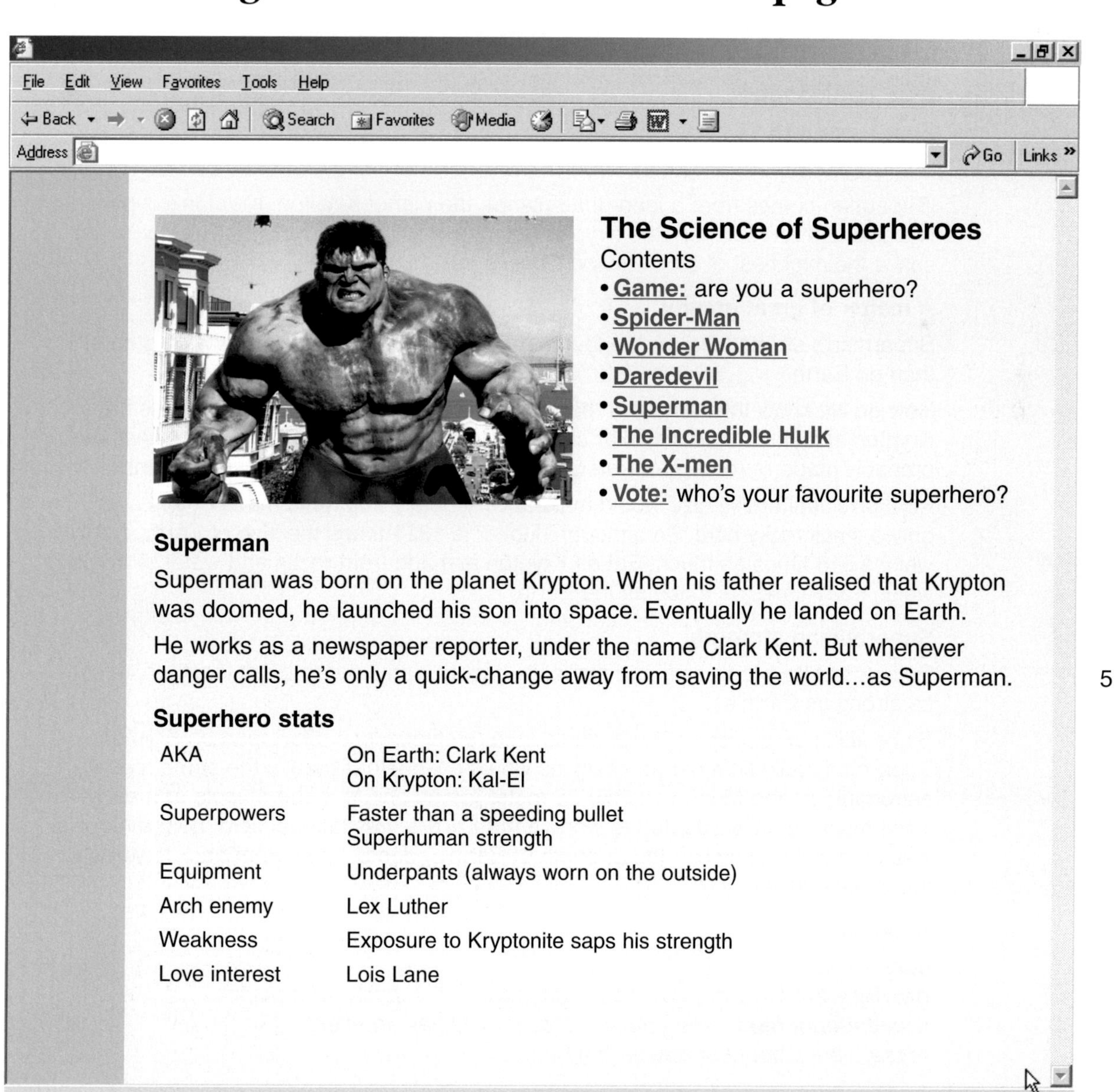


**The Science of Superheroes**

Contents
- **Game:** are you a superhero?
- **Spider-Man**
- **Wonder Woman**
- **Daredevil**
- **Superman**
- **The Incredible Hulk**
- **The X-men**
- **Vote:** who's your favourite superhero?

**Superman**

Superman was born on the planet Krypton. When his father realised that Krypton was doomed, he launched his son into space. Eventually he landed on Earth.

He works as a newspaper reporter, under the name Clark Kent. But whenever danger calls, he's only a quick-change away from saving the world...as Superman.

**Superhero stats**

| | |
|---|---|
| AKA | On Earth: Clark Kent<br>On Krypton: Kal-El |
| Superpowers | Faster than a speeding bullet<br>Superhuman strength |
| Equipment | Underpants (always worn on the outside) |
| Arch enemy | Lex Luther |
| Weakness | Exposure to Kryptonite saps his strength |
| Love interest | Lois Lane |

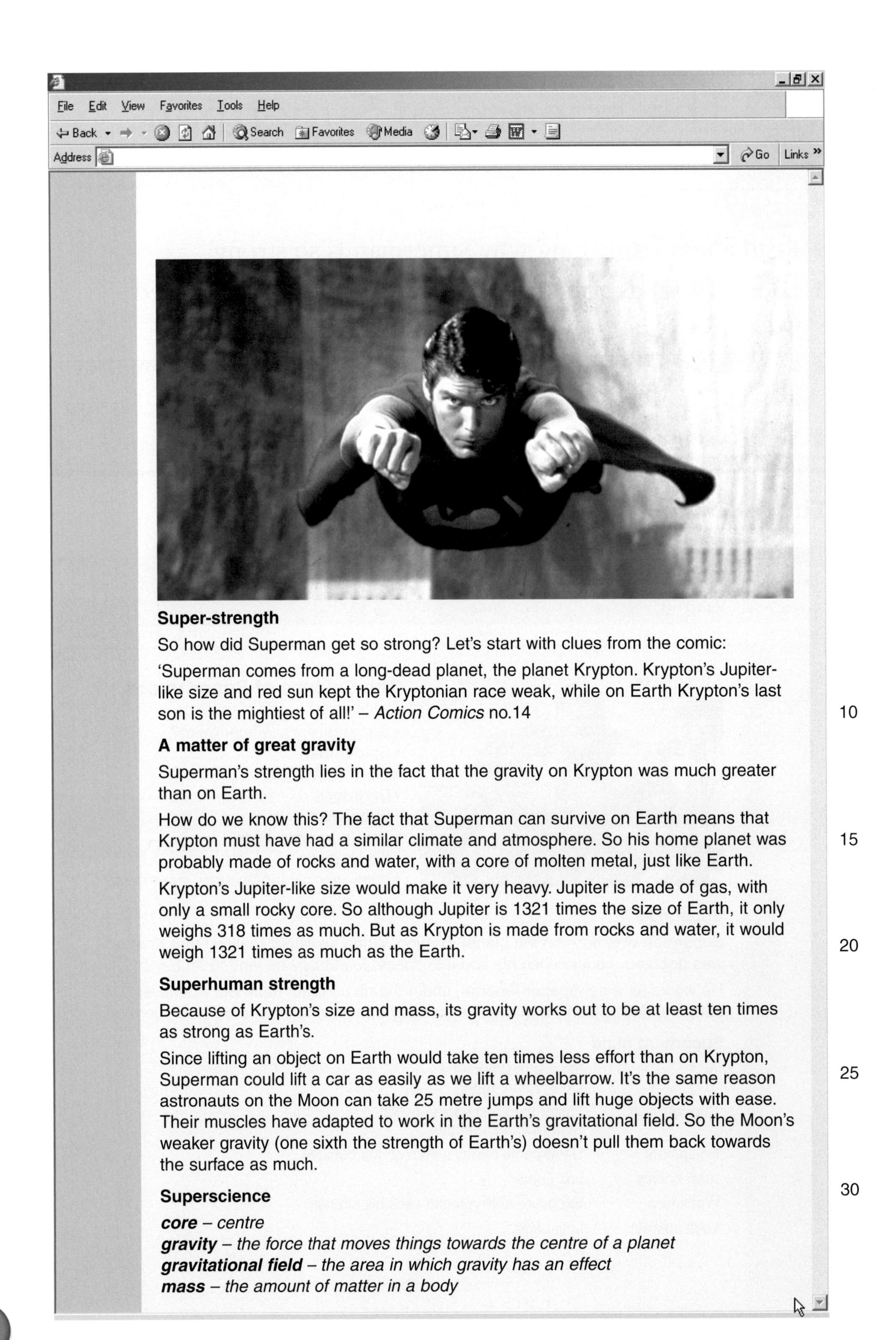


**Super-strength**

So how did Superman get so strong? Let's start with clues from the comic:

'Superman comes from a long-dead planet, the planet Krypton. Krypton's Jupiter-like size and red sun kept the Kryptonian race weak, while on Earth Krypton's last son is the mightiest of all!' – *Action Comics* no.14

**A matter of great gravity**

Superman's strength lies in the fact that the gravity on Krypton was much greater than on Earth.

How do we know this? The fact that Superman can survive on Earth means that Krypton must have had a similar climate and atmosphere. So his home planet was probably made of rocks and water, with a core of molten metal, just like Earth.

Krypton's Jupiter-like size would make it very heavy. Jupiter is made of gas, with only a small rocky core. So although Jupiter is 1321 times the size of Earth, it only weighs 318 times as much. But as Krypton is made from rocks and water, it would weigh 1321 times as much as the Earth.

**Superhuman strength**

Because of Krypton's size and mass, its gravity works out to be at least ten times as strong as Earth's.

Since lifting an object on Earth would take ten times less effort than on Krypton, Superman could lift a car as easily as we lift a wheelbarrow. It's the same reason astronauts on the Moon can take 25 metre jumps and lift huge objects with ease. Their muscles have adapted to work in the Earth's gravitational field. So the Moon's weaker gravity (one sixth the strength of Earth's) doesn't pull them back towards the surface as much.

**Superscience**

***core*** *– centre*
***gravity*** *– the force that moves things towards the centre of a planet*
***gravitational field*** *– the area in which gravity has an effect*
***mass*** *– the amount of matter in a body*

## Key Reading

### Explanation Texts

This text is (mainly) an **explanation**. Its **purpose** is to help someone understand **how** something works, or **why** something has happened.

The main features of an explanation text are:

- It includes a series of **clear and logical steps**. For example: '*Let's start with* clues from the comic' highlights the first step.
- It uses **causal language**, which shows how one thing causes another. For example: '*Because of* Krypton's size and mass, its gravity works out to be at least ten times as strong as Earth's.'
- It uses **precise vocabulary**. For example, technical terms may be explained in a glossary, such as the 'Superscience' section.

**1** Give the **reason** why Superman can lift a car as easily as we lift a wheelbarrow.

**2** What is the **cause** of Superman's strength?

**3** Find two **scientific terms** in this website.

## Purpose

**4** Is the main purpose of *The Science of Superheroes*:

**a)** to explain why Superman is so powerful

**b)** to explain what gravity means

**c)** to give you a fact file on Superman?

## Reading for meaning

**You cannot explain anything well unless your explanation is organised clearly. That is why explanation texts like this one work through a series of points in a clear and logical way.**

**5** The different steps in the explanation are given below in the form of a flow chart. However, they are not in order. Work with a partner to put them in a logical order that matches the extract.

| |
|---|
| **A** So Krypton was probably made of rocks and water, and had a metal core, like Earth. |
| **B** So lifting an object would take Superman ten times less effort than on Krypton. |
| **C** So Krypton must have had the same climate and atmosphere as Earth. |
| **D** So the gravity of Krypton was at least ten times as strong as Earth's. |
| **E** Superman comes from Krypton. But he can survive on Earth. |
| **F** Krypton was the size of Jupiter. Jupiter is 1321 times the size of Earth. |
| **G** So Krypton would have weighed 1321 times as much as Earth. |

**6** Explanation texts have to use words in a precise way. Jot down what exactly the writer means by these words:

**a)** atmosphere (line 15)

**b)** adapted (line 27).

## Focus on: Highlighting cause and effect

Explanation texts give the **reasons why** things happen - or the **causes** of things. Here is an example from the website:

This is the **cause:**
Jupiter is mainly gas

Jupiter is made of gas, with only a small rocky core. *So* although Jupiter is 1321 times the size of Earth, it only weighs 318 times as much.

This is the **effect:** it is only
318 times as heavy as Earth

Causal **connectives** are used to highlight the link between cause and effect. This makes it clear to the reader how the sentences are related. 'So' is the connective in the above example.

### Grammar for reading

A **connective** is a word or phrase that shows the connection between clauses or sentences. You can use many different connectives to highlight cause and effect in explanations: in 'order to', 'when', 'because', 'therefore'.

**7** Scan lines 21–29 to find two different **causal connectives**.

**8** Write out the whole sentence or sentences in each example. Then label the **cause**, the **effect** and the **connective** that highlights the link between the two as in the example above.

## Key Writing

**9** Your task is to **write an explanation** for seven-year-olds of why Spider-Man can walk up walls. Use the pieces of information below to help you. Put them in a clear or logical order and use connectives to highlight each cause and effect.

**A** Spider-Man can stick to almost any surface.

**B** He can shoot silk from 'webslingers' attached to his wrists.

**C** Some spiders release a little bit of sticky silk onto their feet as they move.

**D** The silk anchors their feet in place.

Remember that this explanation is for seven-year-olds. Are any words that you have used too difficult for this audience? Replace them with simpler words.

# 3 Written in the stars?

Aims

- Read a text presenting arguments for and against astrology
- Look at how discursive texts are written and organised (S13f)
- Explore how to help the reader find their way around a text (S8)
- Identify two ways of presenting people's views (R9)
- Practise presenting the views of your classmates (S&L10)

**The word 'myth' is sometimes used to mean a 'made-up' idea.**

## Your stars – science or myth?

'Your love life will take a leap forward this week...but don't make any rash decisions...' Millions of us pore over our horoscopes in newspapers and magazines. But are we just being taken in? *Out Loud* investigates...

### *Putting it to the test!*

5 Many people have tried to prove that astrology is true. To test the astrologers' claim that Mars is the planet of male energy, risk and action, a Frenchman studied the star charts of 570 famous athletes. He was amazed to find that Mars was indeed in key
10 parts of the sky when the athletes were born.

**Fun facts**

- www.doghoroscopes.com is one of hundreds of websites that offer star charts for your pets.
- The earliest horoscope we have is from Babylonia (now Iraq). It dates from 409 BC.
- Each year over a million callers use the 'astroline' phone-ins to find out what the week has in store for them.

But scientists fight back with tests of their own. In 2003 the scientist Geoffrey Dean led his own study of 2000 people born within minutes of one another. He compared more than 100 different features, such as their anxiety levels and artistic
15 ability. And – surprise, surprise – he found that they were not similar in any way.

## For or against?

We asked some of our readers what they thought about astrology.

'I believe in the Bible, not the stars. Astrology is evil.' – Elliott

'Horoscopes? You only see what you want to see in them.' – Ian

'Star signs just pigeonhole people. We're all different, aren't we?' – Kimberly

'Ha ha. You'll be believing in witches next.' – Salman

'I'm a typical Aries – independent and active. It all makes sense to me.' – Greg

'The moon affects the tides, so why can't the planets affect us too?' – Louise

'Science doesn't have all the answers!' – Chenise

'You can't judge on the basis of the star charts in magazines. A true horoscope is based on exactly where and when you were born.' – Raj

## So what's the verdict?
20
## Out Loud *says...*

Hmmm ... a tricky one. We'd love to *believe* in the stars, but that doesn't make it *true*. One thing we can predict, though – the 'science or myth' debate will run and run!

**astrology** the study of the planets and how they affect human behaviour

**horoscope** a birth chart

**verdict** decision

## Key Reading

### Discursive Texts

This article is (mainly) a **discursive** text. Its **purpose** is to help someone understand an issue or debate by presenting the arguments fairly.

The main features of a discursive text are:

- Its **form** consists of an **opening statement**, a **series of points on both sides** of the issue, and a **conclusion**. For example, the first paragraph of the text introduces the issue.
- It has **phrases at the start of sentences** that signal which side of the issue is being written about. For example, '*Many people* have tried to prove that astrology is true'.
- It uses **formal language**. For example, 'To test the astrologers' claim that Mars is the planet of male energy …'.

S13f

**1** What are the **two views** put forward in the text?

**2** Find the first phrase that signals a point of view: 'Millions of us…' (line 2). Is this sentence making a point **for** or **against** astrology? How do you know?

**3** Look at line 11: 'In 2003 the scientist Geoffrey Dean led his own study of 2000 people'. This could have been written as: 'A couple of years ago a boffin called Geoff Dean checked out loads of guys'. Which version is written in more **formal language**?

## Purpose

**4** Is the **main purpose** of this text:

**a)** to entertain readers by presenting information on a hot topic

**b)** to help someone understand both sides of the debate on astrology

**c)** to argue that astrology isn't true?

Give reasons for your answer.

## Reading for meaning

**5** The title of a discursive text is often a question. What question does the **title** of this article ask? Discuss with a partner how you could rewrite the question to make it very clear what the debate is about.

The first paragraph of a discursive text often gives a brief introduction to the issue. This could include:

- background information
- a summary of the arguments on both sides.

**6** What kind of **introduction** does this article have? Point to the evidence in the text for your answer.

**7** What view does *Out Loud* magazine have on astrology (see the last paragraph)?

## Using paragraphs

A discursive text has to be organised very clearly. This is because:

- the writer is giving you **more than one view** on a subject
- each view may be backed up by several **different points**
- the subject itself may be quite complicated!

This is where paragraphs become useful: each paragraph covers a different point. Also, the first sentence usually tells you what the focus or main point of the paragraph is. For example, look at lines 5–10:

**New point:** the writer now discusses 'proof' of astrology. So a **new paragraph** is used to make this point

**First sentence:** makes it clear what the paragraph is about

Many people have tried to prove that astrology is true. To test the astrologers' claim that Mars is the planet of male energy, risk and action, a Frenchman studied the star charts of 570 famous athletes. He was amazed to find that Mars was indeed in key parts of the sky when the athletes were born.

**8** Working in pairs, present the next paragraph in the same way.

**a)** **Write out** the paragraph and state what **new point** is being made.

**b)** How does the **first sentence** make this clear to the reader?

## Focus on: Presenting different views

Discursive texts give the views of people from both sides of the debate. There are two main ways of doing this:

- You can **quote the views directly**:

The **exact words** of the person are given in **inverted commas**

> 'Horoscopes? You only see what you want to see in them.' – Ian

The **person** who said the words is named

Often a verb like 'says' or 'thinks' is used:

> 'Horoscopes? You only see what you want to see in them,' *said* Ian.

- Or you can *report* the views. This means summarising a person's views, without using their actual words:

The **person** or **people** whose views are summarised

The **words** of the person are **reported** (summarised) without using inverted commas

> To test the astrologers' claim that Mars is the planet of male energy, risk and action

There are many phrases that introduce reported speech, for example: 'say that', 'state that', 'argue that', 'believe that'.

**9** Working with a partner:

**a)** Find one other example of a view that is **quoted directly**.

**b)** Find one other example of a view that is **reported**.

**c)** **Present these** to show the two different parts of the sentence, as in the examples above and on the previous page.

## Key Speaking and Listening

**10** In groups of four or five:

**a)** **Discuss** what you think about astrology for two minutes.

**b)** Then each think about how you could state your own view in **one or two sentences**.

**c)** Take it in turns to **state your view**, and **listen** to others' views.

**d)** Finally, take it in turns to **summarise** the discussion.

- Use different phrases to **report** people's views.
- Quote some of your friends' words directly.

# 4 Unit 2 Assignment: What the papers say about *Troy*

## Assessment Focuses

- AF2 Produce texts which are appropriate to task, reader and purpose
- AF4 Construct paragraphs and use cohesion within and between paragraphs

**You:** are a writer for a film magazine.
**Your task:** to write a summary of opinion about the film *Troy* – a 'Review of reviews'.

## Stage 1

On the next page are some notes that you have made about the film *Troy*. Three kinds of notes are mixed up:

- extracts from the film review in *The Morning News*
- extracts from the film review in *The Evening Star*
- background information about the film.

You need the material for three paragraphs of text for your article. Use a chart like the one on page 49 to help you order the points into three paragraphs.

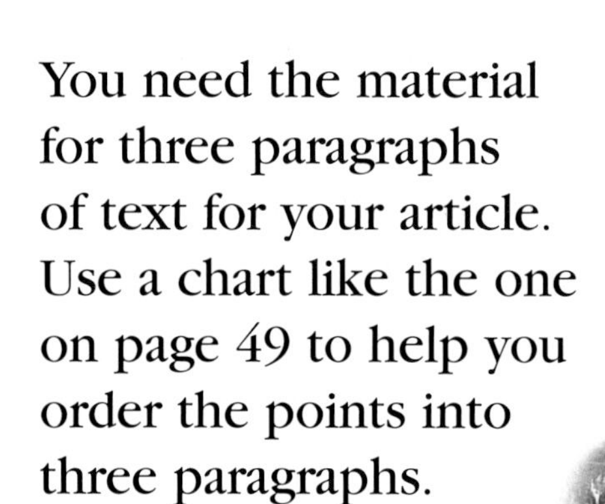

"Brad Pitt is a sulky, beefy hunk. He is perfect as the Greek hero Achilles." (*The Evening Star*)

*Troy* is based on an ancient Greek legend, as told by the poet Homer in the *Iliad*.

"Achilles should be a noble figure, but Brad Pitt reduces him to a lout." (*The Morning News*)

"Troy is terrible. The wooden horse is great, but the wooden acting is not." (*The Morning News*)

Certificate 15, 162 minutes long.

"Give me *Gladiator* any day." (*The Morning News*)

"Movie of the year. This is a Greek version of *Gladiator*." (*The Evening Star*)

'The two and half hours raced by.' (*The Evening Star*)

*Troy* is an adventure film.

"There are spectacular battle sequences, political drama, and romance between Helen (Diane Kruger) and Paris (Orlando Bloom)." (*The Evening Star*)

Troy cost 200 million dollars to make.

"The romance between Paris and Helen is feeble." (*The Morning News*)

| Paragraph 1: Introduction – background | |
|---|---|
| Paragraph 2: *Morning News* – against Troy | **1**<br>**2**<br>**3** |
| Paragraph 3: *Evening Star* – for Troy | **1**<br>**2**<br>**3** |

## Stage 2

Use the material in your chart to **draft three paragraphs of text**. Remember:

- Begin with an **introduction**.
- Give each paragraph a clear **main focus**.
- Use **phrases at the start of a sentence** to signal what point of view you are summarising, for example, '*The Evening Star* is full of praise for the film' or 'Turning to the *Evening Star*, however, …'.
- Don't always **quote directly** from the newspapers. For variety, include some **summaries** in your own words.

# Unit 3 Out of this world

## 1 Alien visitors

### Aims

- Read an extract from a discursive text
- Look at how different points of view are presented
- Look at the way discursive texts are organised (S13f)
- Learn how to assess the content of a text (R8)

**The following text is from a website dealing with the possibility of life on other planets.**

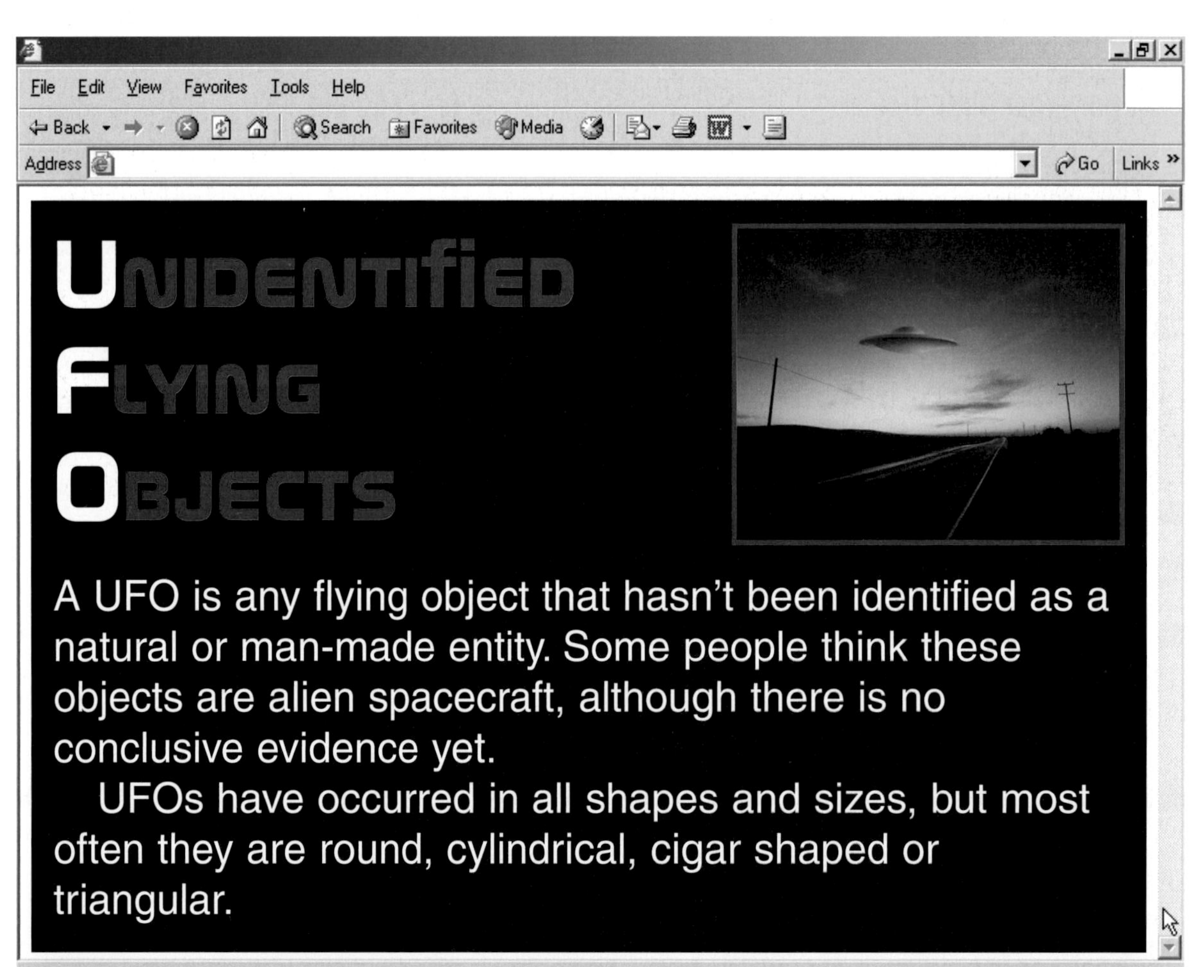


UNIDENTIFIED
FLYING
OBJECTS

A UFO is any flying object that hasn't been identified as a natural or man-made entity. Some people think these objects are alien spacecraft, although there is no conclusive evidence yet.

5 UFOs have occurred in all shapes and sizes, but most often they are round, cylindrical, cigar shaped or triangular.

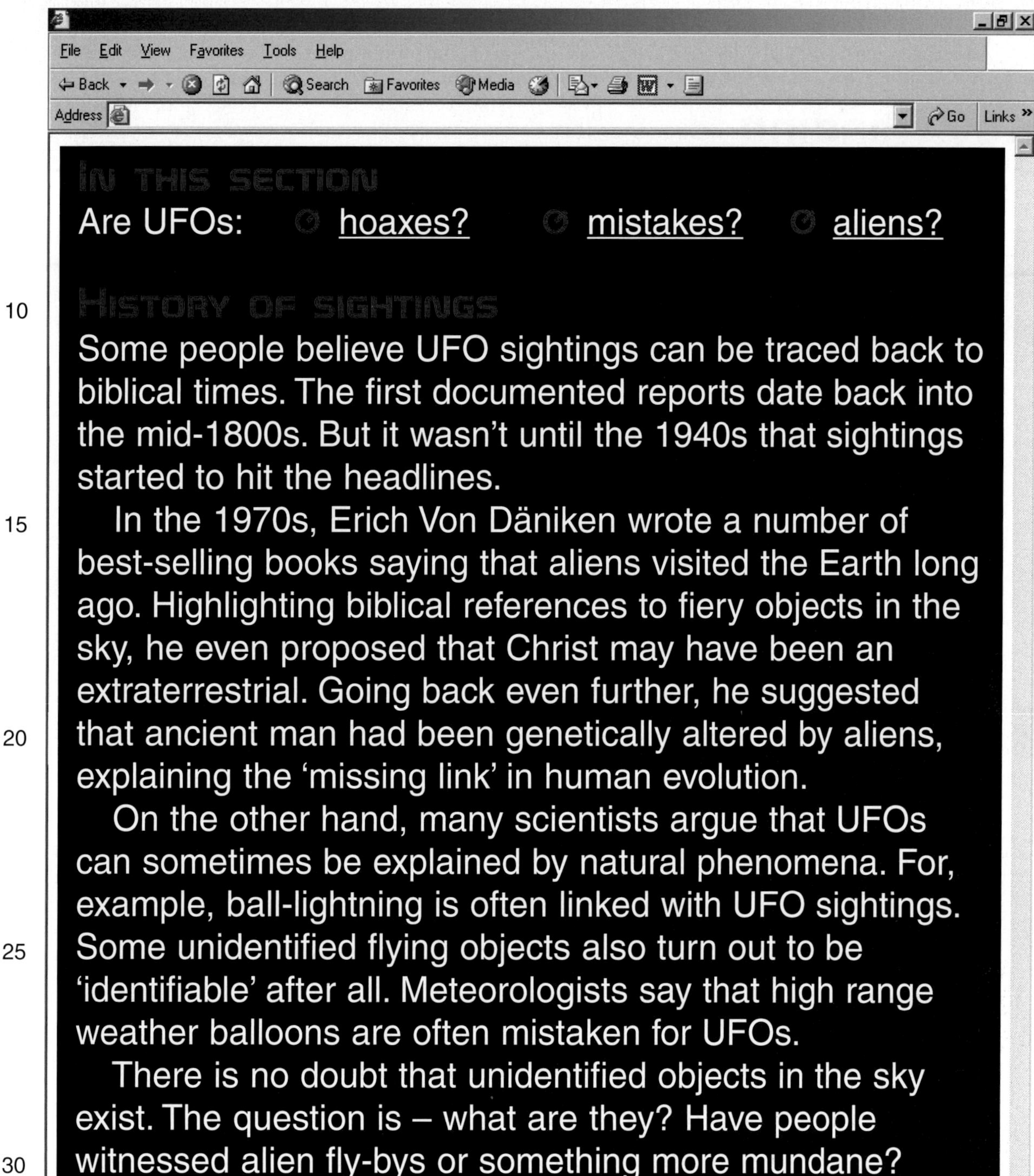


IN THIS SECTION

Are UFOs: hoaxes? mistakes? aliens?

HISTORY OF SIGHTINGS

Some people believe UFO sightings can be traced back to biblical times. The first documented reports date back into the mid-1800s. But it wasn't until the 1940s that sightings started to hit the headlines.

In the 1970s, Erich Von Däniken wrote a number of best-selling books saying that aliens visited the Earth long ago. Highlighting biblical references to fiery objects in the sky, he even proposed that Christ may have been an extraterrestrial. Going back even further, he suggested that ancient man had been genetically altered by aliens, explaining the 'missing link' in human evolution.

On the other hand, many scientists argue that UFOs can sometimes be explained by natural phenomena. For, example, ball-lightning is often linked with UFO sightings. Some unidentified flying objects also turn out to be 'identifiable' after all. Meteorologists say that high range weather balloons are often mistaken for UFOs.

There is no doubt that unidentified objects in the sky exist. The question is – what are they? Have people witnessed alien fly-bys or something more mundane?

**entity** thing
**conclusive** completely convincing
**documented** backed up by written evidence
**biblical references** stories in the Christian Bible
**extraterrestrial** from a planet other than Earth
**genetically altered** changed at the most basic biological level
**phenomena** happenings
**ball-lightning** a globe of glowing electrical current that floats in the air
**mundane** ordinary

## Key Reading

### Discursive texts

This text is **discursive**. Its **purpose** is to present an argument from different points of view.

The main features of a discursive text are:

- A stucture that consists of an **opening statement**, a series of **points** on both sides of the issue, and a **conclusion**. For example, paragraph 1 of the webpage introduces UFOs as the issue for discussion.
- **Connectives** or **linking phrases** that signal which side of the issue you are writing about. For example, 'Some people believe…'
- It is written mainly in the **present** tense. For example, 'A UFO *is* any flying object...'
- It clearly shows **evidence for each viewpoint**. For example, 'Erich Von Däniken wrote...', 'many scientists argue that…'

**1** The extract is written mainly in the present tense but sometimes uses the past tense.

**a)** Find **one example** in paragraph 4 where the **past tense** is used.

**b)** What **kind of information** is being presented?

**2** Find **two pieces of evidence** to suggest that UFOs can be explained from paragraph 5.

**3** Find the linking phrases at the start of paragraphs 3 and 5 which signal that a different point of view will be described.

## Purpose

**4** Choose the **main purpose** of the extract from the following options:

- to convince the reader that UFOs are real
- to entertain the reader with stories of UFOs
- to put forward views from both sides of the debate and leave the reader to decide about UFOs.

A **fact** is something that you can prove to be true or real. An **opinion** is what somebody thinks or believes.

**5** In pairs, decide which parts of the extract give facts and which give opinions.

**a)** Find **two facts** in the extract.

**b)** Find **two opinions**.

**c)** Does the **writer** give his opinion anywhere in the text?

## Reading for meaning

**6** When were the **earliest documented** sightings of UFOs?

**7** According to **some people**, how far back do UFO sightings go?

**8** Find **one example** of how scientists explain UFOs.

**9** What **man-made object** has been the cause of some UFO sightings?

**10** The writer asks two questions at the end of the extract.

**a)** What is the **first question**?

**b)** How does the second question **help the reader** to answer the first question?

## Focus on: Assessing the content of discursive texts

**When assessing a discursive text, you first need to identify the views that are being presented.**

**11** **a)** What are the **two main views** presented in this extract?

**b)** Make **a list of the main points** made for each view. It may help to present them in a chart like the one below:

| View 1 – Points for UFOs | View 2 – Points against UFOs |
|---|---|
| First documented sightings 1880s | Explained by natural phenomena |
| Biblical references to fiery objects in sky | |
| | |

R8 **12** Each main point is backed up by a piece of evidence. **Find the evidence** given for each point you have listed in your chart.

**13** The writer uses several different phrases to introduce different views. These include:

- Some people *think...*
- Erich Von Däniken *wrote...*
- Many scientists *argue...*

**a)** Experiment with these phrases by **replacing the verbs** in italics with some of the following verbs: 'suggest', 'claim', 'insist', 'believe', 'deny'.

**b)** What **difference** does changing the verb make to the strength of the view being expressed?

## Key Writing

**14** a) In pairs, spend five minutes discussing whether there is alien life on other planets. Try to come up with **two main points for** and **two main points against**.

S&L12

You might find these points useful to start you off:

- Frequent UFO sightings in our skies
- No response to any messages sent into space from Earth
- Evidence of water found on Mars
- Scientific explanations for UFO sightings.

b) On your own, **write a discursive piece** of 75–100 words entitled 'Is there life on other planets?'

Here are some words and phrases that might help you:

- 'Some people believe/think...'
- 'Others have suggested...'
- 'Whether there is life on other planets or not...'
- 'The fact is...'

Remember:

- to **start** your piece by saying what your topic is
- to **end** by asking the reader to decide what he or she thinks.

- Read the opening of a story
- Look at the way the text prepares you for the rest of the story (R15)
- Write your own introduction to a story (Wr5)

---

**The following extract is the opening of a novel called *Only You Can Save Mankind* by Terry Pratchett.**

## The Hero with a Thousand Extra Lives

Johnny bit his lip, and concentrated.

Right. Come in quick, let a missile target itself – *beep beep beep beebeebeebeeb* – on the first fighter, fire the missile – *thwump* – empty the guns at the fighter – *fplat fplat fplat fplat* – hit fighter No. 2 and take out its shields with the laser – *bwizzle* – while the missile – *pwwosh* – takes out fighter No. 1, dive, switch guns, rake fighter No. 3 as it turns *fplat fplat fplat* – pick up fighter No. 2 in the sights again up the upcurve, let go a missile – *thwump* – and rake it with –

*Fwit fwit fwit.*

Fighter No.4! It always came in last, but if you went after it first the others would have time to turn and you'd end up in the sights of three of them.

He'd died six times already. And it was only five o'clock.

His hands flew over the keyboard. Stars roared past as he accelerated out of the mêlée. It'd leave him short of fuel, but by the time they caught up the shields would be back and he'd be ready, and two of them would already have taken damage, and .... here they come ... missiles away, wow, lucky hit on the first one, die die die!, red fireball – *swssh* – take shield loss while concentrating fire on the next one – *swssh* – and now the last one was running, but he could outrun it, hit the accelerator – ggrrRRRSSHHH – and just keep it in his sights while he poured shot after shot into – *swssh*.

Ah!

The huge bulk of their capital ship was in the corner of the screen. Level 10, here we come ... careful, careful ... there were no more ships now, so all he had to do was keep out of its range and then sweep in and

*We wish to talk.*

**accelerated** moved faster
**mêlée** confusing crowd
**capital ship** large warship

## Key Reading

### Narrative texts

This text is a **narrative**. Its **purpose** is to begin a **story** in an entertaining way.

The main features of a narrative text are:

- It has a structure that includes an opening (**introduction**), a problem (**complication**), a dramatic moment when everything comes to a head (**crisis**) and an ending (**resolution**) when things are sorted out. Since this is the beginning of a novel, only the **introduction** and **problem** are present. However, we can think about the possible **crisis** and **ending** from the title of the novel – *Only You Can Save Mankind*.
  **Introduction:** We are introduced to Johnny who is playing a computer game.
  **Problem:** The game aliens act in an unexpected way.
  **Crisis:** How will Johnny respond to the aliens?
  **Ending:** How Johnny and the aliens solve their problems.
- It has **characters** who the story is about. We often hear their words and thoughts. For example, in this part of the story, the words of the aliens are shown in italics – '*We wish to talk.*' Johnny's thoughts are also part of the story as he thinks himself through the game: 'Right. Come in quick, let a missile target itself…'
- There is also a **narrator** who tells the story.
- It uses **powerful words**. The narrative must be interesting to read or listen to. For example, 'Stars roared past as he accelerated out of the mêlée.'

**1** The story dives straight into the action of the game. How does the writer's use of **short paragraphs** add to this?

**2** The story uses invented words to create the sounds of the game. Find **three examples** of these words and explain the actions that go with them. For example, 'swssh' = sound of a missile exploding in paragraph 6.

**3** In the extract, sound effects are shown in italics. So are the words of the aliens. How is **direct speech normally shown** in a story?

## Purpose

**The purpose of a story opening is to draw the reader in.**

**4** With a partner, discuss how the extract draws the reader in through:

**a)** how the **main character**, Johnny, is introduced

**b)** the action-packed **start** of the game

**c)** the use of **humour**, for example, 'He'd died six times already. And it was only five o'clock.'

**5** **a)** How clear is it at the start that Johnny is playing a game?

**b)** **At what point** does it become clear?

## Reading for meaning

**6** **How many fighters** must Johnny defeat before he gets to the capital ship?

**7** What **two weapons** does Johnny use against the aliens?

**8** Apart from hitting the aliens, **what else** does Johnny have to think about as he plays the game?

**9** What **level** of the game is Johnny playing at?

### Use of paragraphs

This story opening makes interesting use of very short **paragraphs**. Paragraphs are usually groups of sentences on a particular topic. However, single sentence paragraphs can make part of a text stand out.

**10** In pairs, **discuss these points** about paragraphing in the story.

**a)** What do the very short paragraphs seem to be about?

**b)** Why do you think one word is given a paragraph to itself?

## Focus on: Successful story openings

The opening of a novel is very important. It is vital that it grabs the reader's interest or he or she will not read on.

Some ingredients of a good story opening are:

- Something exciting happens at the start.
- The problem (complication) is set up quickly.
- A piece of action grabs the reader's interest.
- The main character is introduced in an interesting way.

**11** Which of these **techniques** are used in the opening of *Only You Can Save Mankind*?

S&L12

**12** Discuss the following questions with a partner. Decide which of these points help to **involve the reader** in the extract.

**a)** What **kind of story** does the title suggest?

**b)** How does the **chapter heading** 'The Hero with a Thousand Extra Lives' help to suggest a computer game?

**c)** What **features** of a computer game are included in the story?

**d)** Why is the message '*We wish to talk*' so **unexpected**?

Be prepared to report your ideas to the rest of the class.

R15

**13** How many **clues** does the opening of *Only You Can Save Mankind* give about how the story will develop?

Below are some ways in which the story might develop. Choose what you consider to be the best from these options. Refer to clues from the extract to support your ideas.

- Johnny will respond to the aliens' message.
- Johnny will help to save the world.
- Johnny will ignore the aliens' message.

## Key Writing

**14 a)** Use the table below to help you **plan an exciting opening** to a story.

| | |
|---|---|
| An interesting title | |
| Start with an exciting piece of action | |
| Set up a problem (complication) quickly | |
| Include an event that grabs the reader's attention | |
| Introduce the main character(s) in an interesting way | |

**b)** Show your plan to a partner. Ask your partner how he or she thinks the story will develop.

**c)** Write your story opening in **four to five paragraphs**.

# Real aliens

## Aims

- Read a text about aliens
- Think about audiences for texts
- Look at how information texts are put together (S13a)
- Compose your own information text (Wr10)

**The following text is from a book about life on other planets.**

### Alien Life

The features of living things on Earth have arisen by evolution – a long, slow process by which living things adapt to their environment. Feathers, leaves, flowers, legs, feet and eyes, and even blood and bones, have evolved over millions of years in the particular conditions found here on Earth. So it's unlikely that on other planets there are creatures which look like donkeys or slugs. Flowers and trees are likely to be unique to Earth too.

So alien life probably wouldn't look anything like the plants and animals that we know. And it is even less likely to resemble human beings. Jack Cohen, an evolutionary biologist and author, says that he doesn't believe UFO stories about little green men – not because they are little and green, but because they are men. It is unlikely, though not impossible, that aliens would be humanoid as they so often are described in stories of close encounters.

Can we make any guesses about what alien life might look like? Living things on other planets will probably have evolved to suit their environment, as they have done on Earth. But the conditions on other planets or

moons are likely to be quite different to those on Earth, so any life there would also be very different. Life on
25 Earth depends on a mixture of nitrogen, oxygen, carbon dioxide and water vapour, but another planet's atmosphere might contain lots of methane and ammonia gases, or a mist of sulphuric acid.

A large planet has a stronger gravitational pull than a
30 small one. Creatures living on such a planet wouldn't survive well with long, thin legs. Perhaps small creatures would evolve there.

Sulphuric acid can be highly corrosive. On a planet with sulphuric acid in the atmosphere, no creature like
35 any on Earth would survive. A thick, outer covering would be a must for any living thing there.

Some planets have no real surface at all – they are made of gases. Jupiter and Saturn are examples of such 'gas giants' in our own Solar System. Living things on
40 this planet would have to be buoyant, like a hot air balloon, or have wings to stop themselves from falling down to the hot, dense centre of the planet.

**environment** natural surroundings
**unique** unlike anything else
**humanoid** shaped like human beings
**close encounters** meetings with aliens
**gravitational pull** the force that causes things to have weight
**corrosive** causing damage by chemical action
**buoyant** able to float

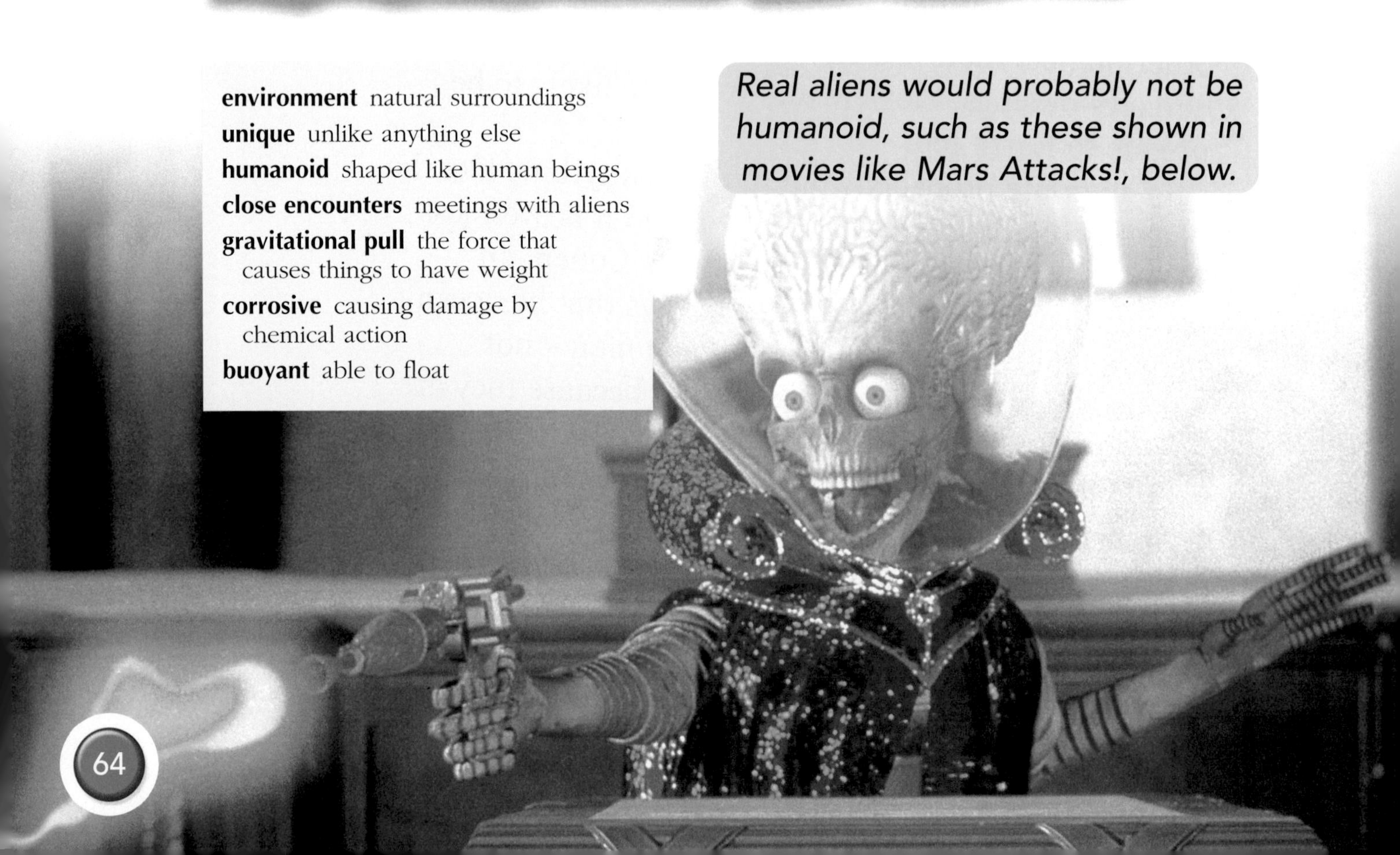

*Real aliens would probably not be humanoid, such as these shown in movies like Mars Attacks!, below.*

## Key Reading

### Explanation texts

This text is (mainly) an **explanation**. Its **purpose** is to help someone understand *how* something might work or *why* something could happen.

The main features of an explanation text are:

- It has a series of **clear and logical steps**. For example, 'The features of living things on Earth have arisen by evolution', highlights the first point to be explained.
- It has **causal language** that shows how one thing causes another. For example, '*So* alien life probably wouldn't look anything like…'
- It has **precise vocabulary**; technical terms may be explained in a glossary. For example, 'stronger *gravitational pull*'.
- It often has **illustrations** or **diagrams** to illustrate points being explained.

**1** Give the **reason** why it is unlikely that you find 'donkeys or slugs' on another planet (paragraph 1).

**2** What short **connective** is used to show the logical conclusions in paragraphs 1 and 2?

**3** Find three more **scientific terms** in the explanation.

#### Grammar for reading

**Connectives** are words that show how one sentence or clause is connected to another. For example, 'and', 'so', 'therefore' or 'but'.

## Purpose

The purpose of this explanation text is to explain some complex ideas about how life forms develop, in a simple way.

**4** With a partner, discuss how well the text explains these ideas. Think about its use of:

**a) examples** to illustrate each point

**b) connectives** to point to key ideas.

*ET – another humanoid alien.*

## Reading for meaning

**5** By which **process** did life develop on Earth?

**6** Why might life forms be **different** on different planets?

**7** What **kinds of alien** life would you expect on a planet with strong gravity?

**8** What life forms might you find on a planet made up of **gases**?

## Focus on: The structure of an explanation text

This explanation text is organised to show the reader a clear and logical progression of ideas. The flow chart on page 67 shows how the main ideas in the text are ordered.

Life on Earth developed through evolution.

Life on Earth developed to fit in with Earth's conditions.

Life on other planets will be different.

Examples of how life on other planets might fit into the environments there.

**9** In groups, discuss how you could arrange the ideas in the flowchart into a **different order**. For example, could you begin with the idea of different life forms for different planets?

**10** Unlike most scientific explanations, this extract is about something that may not exist. The writer makes use of language that shows the **possibility** of these ideas, such as: 'might be', 'perhaps', 'it's unlikely that', 'probably', 'is likely to be', 'would be'.

**a)** **Find these phrases** in the extract.

**b)** Make a note of the **main idea** that each word or phrase is linked to.

## Key Writing

**12** Write a short explanation about one of these things that doesn't actually exist:

- my ideal room
- my ideal school
- my ideal holiday.

You will need to explain:

- what the thing you are describing might **look** like
- what would make it **special**
- what its **advantages** would probably be.

# ④ Unit 3 Assignment: Science writing

## Assessment Focuses

- AF3 Organise and present whole texts effectively, sequencing and structuring information, ideas and events

---

**You:** are a science writer.

**Your task:** to write an explanation text for an encyclopaedia about an alien of your own invention.

**Your audience:** young teenagers.

**You need to decide:**

- how you will address your audience
- how formal your language will be
- whether diagrams will be useful.

## Stage 1

First, you need to choose an alien from one of these planets:

- a planet with very light gravity
- a very dark planet
- a planet with intense radiation problems
- a planet with a poor atmosphere.

Make notes about how your alien has adapted to the conditions on its planet. Then make a sketch of how your alien might look. Draw your alien on its home planet.

## Stage 2

Think about how to organise the ideas in your text. Include:

- a brief introduction on why life forms will be different on different planets
- a description of how your alien looks
- an explanation of how your alien has adapted to the conditions on its planet
- a labelled illustration of your alien.

## Stage 3

Remember to use the language of an explanation text. Include:

- **causal language** that shows how one thing causes another
- **precise vocabulary** and **technical terms** that may be explained in the text.

Now add words and phrases that **express the possibility** of your ideas, such as: 'might be', 'unlikely to be', 'would be', 'probably' and 'possibly'.

# Unit 4 A life of crime

## 1 Camp Green Lake

- Read an extract from the story *Holes*
- Learn about story openings
- Learn what 'literal' and 'inference' means (R8)
- Learn how the writer keeps the reader interested (R12, Wr7)
- Write a story opening (Wr5, Wr14)

---

**This is the beginning of the story *Holes* by Louis Sachar. It is set in Texas. As you read it, try to imagine what Camp Green Lake is like.**

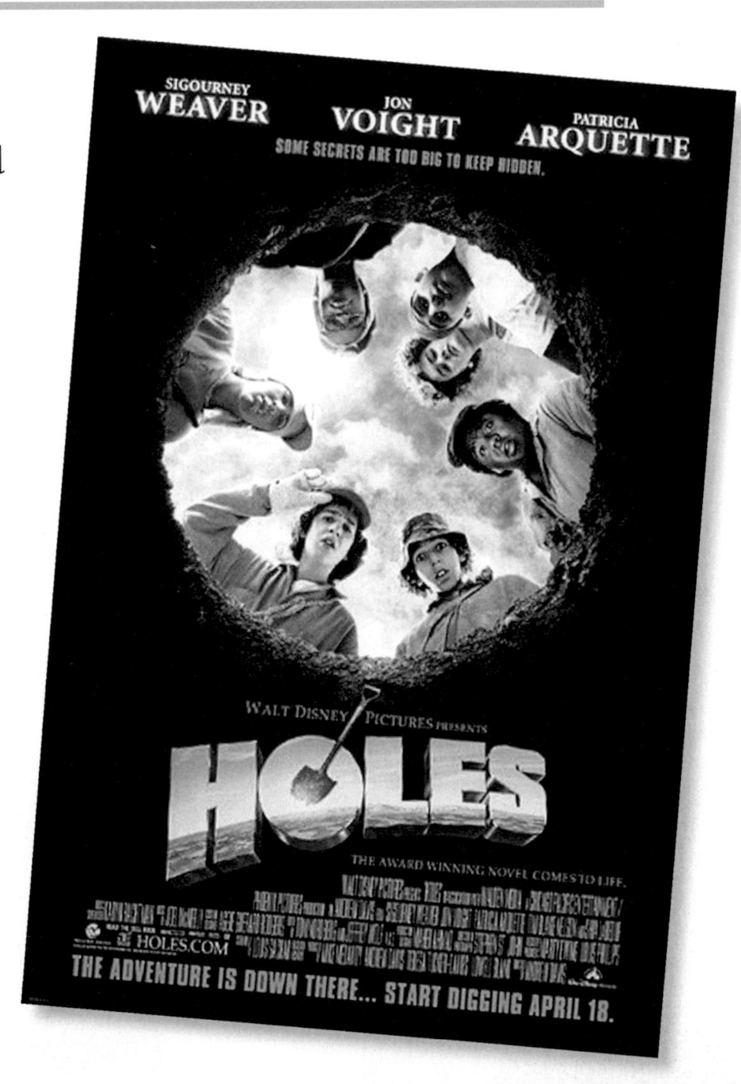

# Holes

## 1

There is no lake at Camp Green Lake. There was once a very large lake here, the largest in Texas. That was over a hundred years ago. Now it is just a dry, flat wasteland.

There used to be a town of Green Lake as well. The town shrivelled and dried up along with the lake, and the people who lived there.

During the summer the daytime temperature hovers around ninety-five degrees in the shade – if you can find any shade. There's not much shade in a big dry lake.

The only trees are two old oaks on the eastern edge of the "lake." A hammock is stretched between the two trees, and a log cabin stands behind that.

The campers are forbidden to lie in the hammock. It belongs to the Warden. The Warden owns the shade.

Out on the lake, rattlesnakes and scorpions find shade under rocks and in the holes dug by the campers.

Here's a good rule to remember about rattlesnakes and scorpions: If you don't bother them, they won't bother you.

Usually.

Sometimes a camper will try to be bitten by a scorpion, or even a rattlesnake. Then he will get to spend a day or two recovering in his tent, instead of having to dig a hole out on the lake.

But you don't want to be bitten by a yellow-spotted lizard. You might as well go into the shade of the oak trees and lie in the hammock.

There is nothing anyone can do to you anymore.

## 2

The reader is probably asking: Why would anyone go to Camp Green Lake?

Most campers weren't given a choice. Camp Green Lake is a camp for bad boys.

If you take a bad boy and make him dig a hole every day in the hot sun, it will turn him into a good boy.

That was what some people thought.

Stanley Yelnats was given a choice. The judge said, "you may go to jail, or you may go to Camp Green Lake."

Stanley was from a poor family. He had never been to a camp before.

**warden** person in charge

**hammock** a simple bed made of canvas, with cords at the end. Often hung between the branches of two trees

# Key Reading

## Narrative Texts

This text is a **story opening** from a **narrative**. The **purpose** of a **narrative** is to entertain us. Its main features are:

- A structure that includes an opening (**introduction**), a problem (**complication**), a dramatic moment when everything comes to a head (**crisis**), and an ending (**resolution**) when things are sorted out.
- **Characters**, who the story is about. We often hear their words and thoughts.
- There is also a **narrator**, who tells the story. For example, in *Holes* the narrator gives the reader a tip: 'Here's a good rule to remember about rattlesnakes and scorpions…'
- **Powerful words**. The narrative must be interesting to read or listen to. For example, 'The town shrivelled and dried up along with the lake.'

**Story openings** describe one of these:

- a character
- a place (**setting**)
- something happening (an **event**).

**1** What kind of **story opening** is used for *Holes*? Choose from the kinds listed above.

**2** The writer uses a range of tenses in Chapter 1. For example:
- past tense: 'There **was** once a very large lake…'
- present tense: 'There **is** no lake at Camp Green Lake.'

Find an example of **each tense** in Chapter 2.

## Purpose

The **purpose** of a story opening is to make the reader keep on reading.

**3** Which of these comments applies to Camp Green Lake in Chapter 1?

- It describes a place that seems familiar
- It leaves you wondering about what kind of place it is.

Wr7

**4** **a)** Find **three things** that the reader is told about Camp Green Lake in paragraph 1.

**b)** What important information is the reader **not** told about Camp Green Lake until Chapter 2?

## Reading for meaning

When a story opens with a setting, the reader needs to feel as if he or she is there. The writer may create powerful pictures (**images**) by using nouns, adjectives and verbs. These describe the scene and set the mood or **tone**. Look at how Camp Green Lake is described:

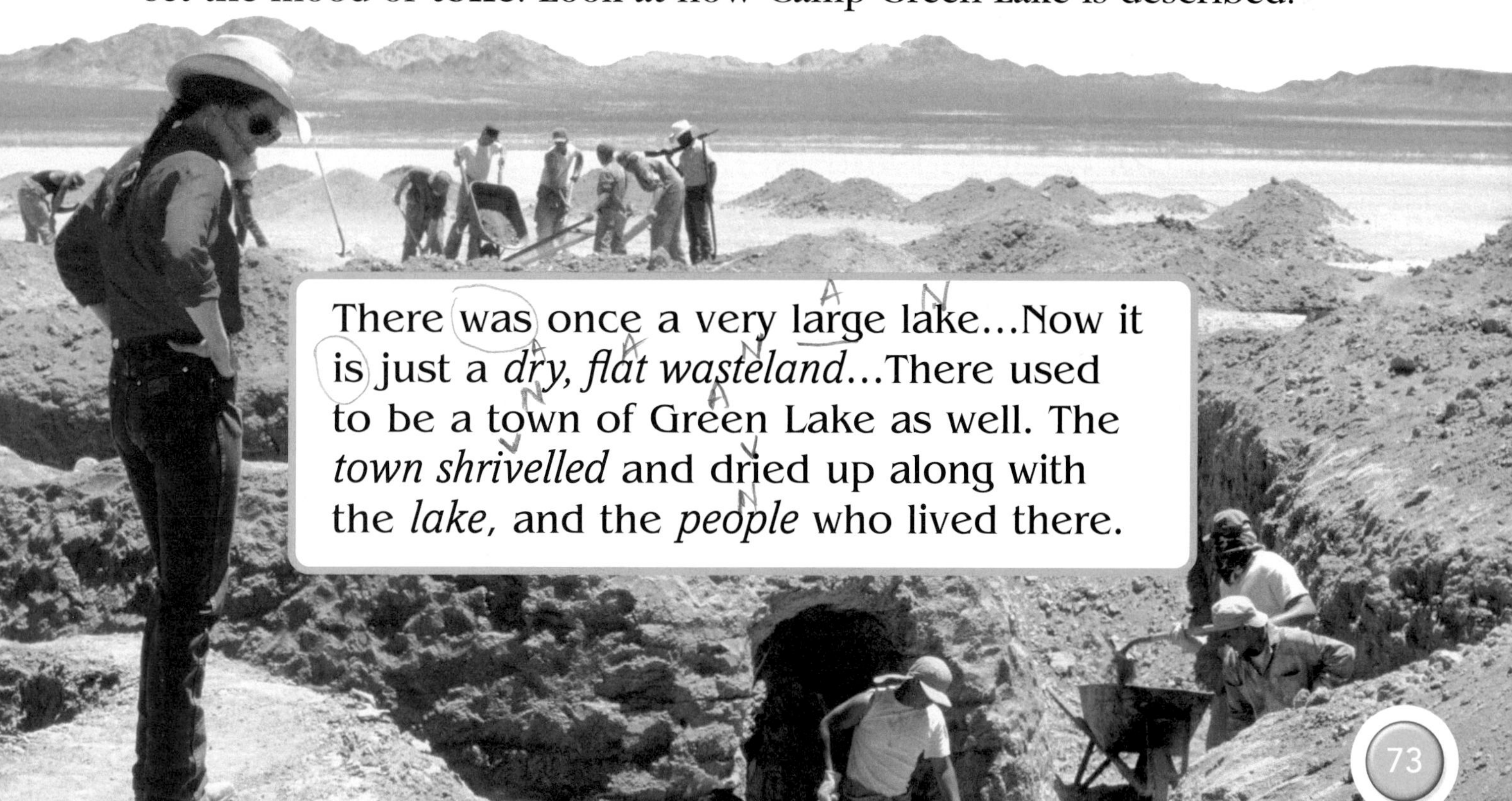

> There was once a very large lake...Now it is just a *dry, flat wasteland*...There used to be a town of Green Lake as well. The *town shrivelled* and dried up along with the *lake*, and the *people* who lived there.

The chart below shows the types of words that appear in *italics*:

| Noun | Adjective | Verb |
|---|---|---|
| wasteland | dry | shrivelled |
| town | flat | |
| lake | | |
| people | | |

R12

**5** a) **Draw a chart** like the one above. Write down only the **nouns** that are listed

b) Choose **three adjectives and verbs** from the list below that have similar meanings to the three in the chart.

| **Adjectives** | | **Verbs** | |
|---|---|---|---|
| fertile | rolling | dwindled | spread |
| stale | dull | shrunk | withered |
| lush | arid | grew | swelled |
| fruitful | humdrum | died | scorched |
| barren | | evaporated | |

- When you have found alternative words, read them in the sentences first, to see if they sound right.
- Remember, you need to find verbs and adjectives to suit *the town, the lake* and *the people*.

## Focus on: Knowing and inferring

When you read a text there is usually information you can be sure of. This is **literal** information. For example:

> Out on the lake, rattlesnakes and scorpions find shade under rocks and in the holes dug by the campers.

However, you may have to pick up clues or **infer** what other information means:

> Here's a good rule to remember about rattlesnakes and scorpions: If you don't bother them, they won't bother you.
> Usually.

The word 'usually' suggests that not only can people be bitten, but they *might* be. In other words, it infers 'danger'.

R8

**6** **a)** Read the following extract from *Holes*.

> But you don't want to be bitten by a yellow-spotted lizard. You might as well go into the shade of the oak trees and lie in the hammock.
> There is nothing anyone can do to you anymore.

**b)** What do you **infer** will happen from the last line of the extract?

We have seen that sometimes the writer will hold back important information. Remember that we are not told that Camp Green Lake is really a prison camp until Chapter 2. However, we are given clues in Chapter 1 that all is not well.
For example, we are told that the campers:

- 'are forbidden to lie in the hammock'
- 'will try to be bitten by a scorpion… instead of having to dig a hole'.

So, from **evidence** in the passage we **infer** that: *The campers seem to be having a hard time.*

**7** **Finish these statements** using **evidence** in Chapter 1:

- The warden seems...
- The wildlife seems...

## Key Writing

**8** Write about **ten sentences** for a story opening with a setting.

- It should describe a room that is in fact a jail. Do not reveal it is a jail until the last sentence.
- Try to make the room sound pleasant but give clues that it is a jail. For example:
  – it could be small but clean
  – the sun could be pouring in through a little window.

**a)** Begin by making a list of things about your cell.
Use nouns and adjectives like this: 'fresh, white walls', 'dazzling sunlight'.

**b)** Think of a starter sentence about your room that sounds positive. For example, 'Although my room is small, it is...'

**c)** When you get towards the end of your story opening, write at least two sentences that suggest things are not quite what they seem. For example, 'Of course, my door is always locked.'

Remember: your final sentence will state the truth.

#  Should music take the rap?

- Read an example of discursive writing
- Use key words to find the main points (R7)
- Use key words to find different points of view
- Learn how to list points in a table
- Write your own point of view

**Read the following article from the BBC Collective website.**

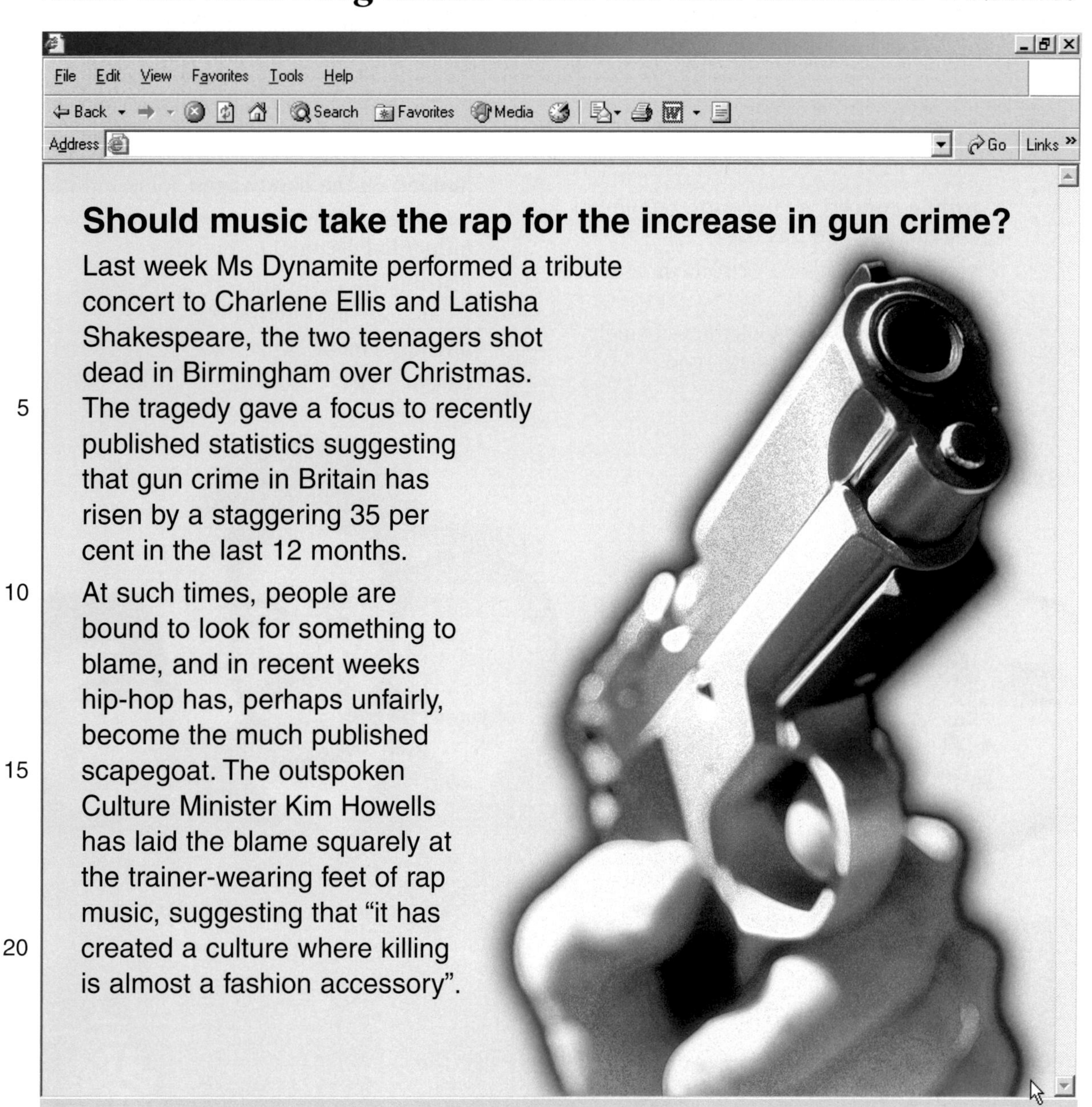


## Should music take the rap for the increase in gun crime?

Last week Ms Dynamite performed a tribute concert to Charlene Ellis and Latisha Shakespeare, the two teenagers shot dead in Birmingham over Christmas. The tragedy gave a focus to recently published statistics suggesting that gun crime in Britain has risen by a staggering 35 per cent in the last 12 months.

At such times, people are bound to look for something to blame, and in recent weeks hip-hop has, perhaps unfairly, become the much published scapegoat. The outspoken Culture Minister Kim Howells has laid the blame squarely at the trainer-wearing feet of rap music, suggesting that "it has created a culture where killing is almost a fashion accessory".

The Home Secretary, David Blunkett, has also jumped on the bandwagon, stating in a recent interview, "I am concerned that we need to talk to the record producers, to the distributors, to those who are actually engaged in the music business about what is and isn't acceptable..."

Blunkett has also been widely condemned for using music as an excuse for a much bigger problem. John Pandit of Asian Dub Foundation and Community Music believes: "If David Blunkett spent as much time looking at the situations that cause crime – drugs, unemployment, bad housing and lack of opportunities – then you might see a difference in the crime figures."

Quest Love, of influential hip-hop act The Roots, agrees: "Do I blame hip-hop for guns and violence? No. But do I blame society for making hip-hop that way? Yes. Should hip-hop be more responsible with its outlook? Yes."

**tribute concert** a concert to remember someone who has died

**scapegoat** someone or something that is unfairly blamed

**fashion accessory** something (usually worn) in an up-to-date style

**jumped on the bandwagon** joined in the popular view

**influential** listened to by others

**distributors** companies that get goods (such as CDs) into shops

**unemployment** no work

**censor** ban

Asian Dub Foundation

# Key Reading

## Discursive texts

This text is a **discursive** text. The **purpose** of discursive writing is to present an **argument** from different points of view.

The main features of a discursive text are:

- A structure that consists of an opening **statement**, a series of **points** on both sides of the issue supported by **evidence**, and a **conclusion**.
- **Phrases at the start of sentences** that **signal** which side of the issue the author is writing about. For example, 'Quest Love, of…The Roots, agrees…'
- **Formal language** in the **present tense**. For example, '…people *are bound* to look…'

**1** What is the subject being discussed in the article? Use the phrase 'whether or not' in your answer.

**2** In what **tense** are the highlighted verbs?

**a)** 'Sometimes society *is* ugly…'

**b)** '…Ms Dynamite *performed* a tribute concert…'

**c)** '…*give* it more resources…'

## Purpose

The **title** of a text can tell us what it is about. Finding **key words** can help us to do this.

The key words of the article's title are shown in *italics*:

> **Should *music* take the *rap* for the *increase* in *gun crime*?**

**3** a) The key word 'rap' has two meanings. Choose the **two meanings** from the following options:

- slap
- blame
- rap music
- chat
- dancing

b) **Write a sentence** to explain what the title really means. Start it like this:

*I think the text is about whether or not…*

## Reading for meaning

The **opening paragraph** of a discursive text is often used to present the **main points**. The opening paragraph of the article tells us several things:

- Ms Dynamite performed a tribute concert.
- The concert was for Charlene and Latisha.
- Charlene and Latisha were shot dead in Birmingham.
- Gun crime has risen by 35 per cent.

How can you tell what the focus of the paragraph is? The writer has used **linking phrases** to show this.

> The tragedy gave a *focus* to…
>
> gun crime in Britain has risen by a staggering 35 per cent…

The phrase links Charlene and Latisha's death with the 'focus' that 'gun crime has risen by…35 per cent…'

Remember, **key words** and **linking phrases** can help us to find the main points in a discursive text.

R7

**4** **a) Read the following extract** from the second paragraph of the article.

> At such times, people are bound to look for something to blame, and in recent weeks hip-hop has, perhaps unfairly, become the much published scapegoat.

**b)** Search for **key words** that tell you the main point. You may wish to use the glossary on page 78.

**c)** Use the key words to **explain to a partner** what the main point of the article is.

**d)** Find the **linking phrase** that connects the second paragraph with the first paragraph.

## Focus on: Points of view

In the article, people give their points of view about whether or not rap is the cause of the increase in gun crime. For example, there are key words that tell us what Kim Howells thinks in paragraph 2:

> ...[rap] has created a culture where killing is almost a fashion accessory.

**5** Does Kim Howells think that rap music is the cause of an increase in gun crime?

**6** a) **Draw up a chart** like the one below. Write 'Kim Howells' in either the 'Agrees' or 'Disagrees' column.

b) Then **write what he says** in the third column.

| Is rap the cause of an increase in gun crime? | | |
|---|---|---|
| **Agrees** | **Disagrees** | **What he or she says** |
| | | |
| | | |

R1

**7** a) Look at paragraph 3. Does David Blunkett agree with Kim Howells or not? Find **key words** that tell you what his point of view is.

b) Put David Blunkett's view under the **correct heading** in the chart.

**8** Look through the rest of the article and identify different people's points of view. **Complete the chart** to show:

a) whether each person agrees or disagrees with the argument that rap is the cause of an increase in gun crime

b) what he or she says.

## Key Writing

**9** **a)** Do you think that rap music is the cause of an increase in gun crime? Think about the different points of view made in the article, both for and against this argument.

**b)** **Complete the writing frame** below.

**Guns and Rap**

Some people think that ...

___

This is because ...

___

Others disagree. They think that ...

___

This is because ...

___

My own point of view is that ...

___

I also think that ...

___

# 3 The trial of Derek Drew

## Aims

- Read the poem, *The Trial of Derek Drew*
- Learn about the form of the poem (R14)
- Learn about formal and informal language (S15)
- Write and perform a poem (Wr8, S&L3)

---

**In this poem by Allan Ahlberg, Derek Drew is always in trouble.**

### THE TRIAL OF DEREK DREW

*The charges*
Derek Drew:
For leaving his reading book at home.
For scribbling his handwriting practice.
5 For swinging on the pegs in the cloakroom.
For sabotaging the girls' skipping.
For doing disgusting things with his dinner.

*Also charged*
Mrs Alice Drew (née Alice Jukes):
10 For giving birth to Derek Drew.
Mr Dennis Drew:
For aiding and abetting Mrs Drew.
Mrs Muriel Drew and Mr Donald Drew:
For giving birth to Dennis Drew, etc.
15 Mrs Jane Jukes and Mr Paul Jukes:
For giving birth to Alice Jukes, etc.
Previous generations of the Drew and Jukes families:
For being born, etc., etc.

*Witnesses*
20 'He's *always* forgetting his book.' Mrs Pine.
'He *can* write neatly, if he wants to.' Ditto.
'I seen him on the pegs, Miss!'
'And me!' 'And me!' Friends of the accused.
'He just kept jumpin' in the rope!' Eight third-year girls
25 In Miss Hodge's class.
'It was disgusting!' Mrs Foot (dinner-lady).

*For the Defence*
'I was never *in* the cloakroom!' Derek Drew

*Mitigating circumstances*
30 This boy is ten years old.
He asks for 386 other charges to be taken into consideration.
'He's not like this at home,' his mother says.

*The Verdict*
Guilty.

35 *The sentence*
Life!
*And* do his handwriting again.

**sabotaging** breaking or damaging something deliberately

**née** born, meaning the name you are born with

**aiding and abetting** helping in a crime

**generations** family members who lived many years before you

**accused** the person on trial

**For the Defence** the reasons given for the behaviour of the accused

**Mitigating circumstances** taking the accused's situation into account

**verdict** decision on whether the accused is guilty

**sentence** punishment if found guilty

## Key Reading

### Poetry

This text is a **poem**. Its **purpose** is to explore feelings and ideas.

A poem is made up of **images**, **rhythm** and **form**.

- The **images** are the pictures made by the words.
- The **rhythm** is like the beat in music.
- The **form** is the framework or pattern of the poem. Poems are written in **lines** not sentences.

Poems can be written in different styles:

- Some poems **rhyme**. For example, doom/gloom/tomb.
- Some poems are **free verse**. They have lines of different lengths with different rhythms. (Although some ree verse contains rhyme.)

Poets use all kinds of ideas to give a poem a framework or form. For example:

- a poem about a spider might be written in the shape of a spider's web
- a poem could be written as a list of instructions, like this poem about the birth of a river:

  First gather morning rain
  Splash down mountainside
  Tip into…

**1** **a)** Read the **sub-headings** above each verse in *The Trial of Derek Drew*. (The first sub-heading is 'The charges'.)

**b)** Where would you expect to find this **kind of language** used?

**2** What kind of **framework** has the poet used?

- a trial in a court
- appearing in front of the school governors.

## Purpose

*The Trial of Derek Drew* explores all the things that Derek has done wrong at school. However, it is a funny or **comic** poem. Why do you think this is?

**3** **a)** Look at the **first verse**, 'The charges', which tells you what Derek has done wrong.

**b)** Would you call what Derek has done '**crimes**'? Why or why not?

**c)** Think about what Derek has done and **write a sentence** to explain why the poem is a comic poem, starting like this: 'I think putting Derek on trial is comic because...'

## Reading for meaning

### Formal and informal language

*The Trial of Derek Drew* uses **official language** to make it seem as if Derek is in a court of law. It is the kind of language used in legal documents:

- Words are often repeated in lists.
- To avoid repeating words, shorthand is sometimes used. For example, 'etc.' (*et cetera*, which means 'and so on').

**4** What word is **constantly repeated** in verses 1 and 2?

**5** **a)** Find another word that is used as **shorthand** in place of a name in verse 3.

**b)** What do you think it means? **Check your answer** in a dictionary.

Using this kind of official language gives us a clear picture of Derek on trial. This image adds to the humour of the poem. However, there is also **informal language** in the poem when people use their own words.

S15

**6** Reread verse 3.

a) **Why** are people speaking here?

b) **Who** are they talking about?

c) **How** can you tell it is in their own words?

Wr8

## Focus on: Shaping a poem

You can use *The Trial of Derek Drew* as a model when writing your own poem.

**7** a) Think of **five things** that would get you into trouble at school or at home. (You can make them up if you wish.)

b) Write down **the first wrong thing** under the heading 'The charges'. For example, if you had left your schoolbag on the bus, you would write:

> *The charges*
> For leaving my schoolbag on the bus.

Remember to begin each line with the word 'For'.

c) **Complete your list** of five charges.

**8** a) Now think of a **defence** (or excuse) for each crime. (Derek has only one). For example, in defence of the schoolbag 'crime' you could write:

> *For the Defence*
> 'I fell asleep.'

**b)** **Complete your list** of reasons for the Defence. At the end of your 'Defence list', write **your name**.

**9** **a)** To finish your poem, decide on '**The verdict**' and '**The sentence**' and write them down.

**b)** Remember to give your poem a **title**.

## Key Speaking and Listening

S&L3 

**10** **a)** In a group, **choose one of your poems** to perform.

**b)** Organise how you are going to present it. One of you will need to introduce the poem, giving the title and the writer's name.

**c)** Then decide which people will read the charges, the verdict, the sentence and the defence (who is the obvious person for this last role?).

**d)** Next, think about the **actual performance**.

- Decide whether you will **sit** or **stand**.
- Do you need any **props**? (If you sit down you will need chairs.)
- What **voices** will you use? (For example, the judge who reads the verdict and the sentence should not sound the same as the person on trial.) If you act out more than one role, how will your voice change?
- As you practise, try to use some of the new **vocabulary** you have learned, for example: 'charges', 'defence'.
- Finally, **run through** your performance before you present it.

# ④ Unit 4 Assignment: The storyteller

## Assessment Focuses

- AF4 Construct paragraphs and use cohesion within and between paragraphs
- AF7 Select appropriate and effective vocabulary

**You:** are a storyteller.

**Your task:** to write a story for other students to read.

## Stage 1

Open your story with a setting.

| | |
|---|---|
| **Where?** | A loft in a deserted old house. |
| **What is it like?** | It has a large, heavy door. It has a small window (skylight) in the roof. It is full of boxes and cases. |
| **What else?** | Think of two more things. |

Then introduce your character.

| | |
|---|---|
| **Who?** | Your character is a criminal. What is his or her name? What age is your character? What is he or she like?* Is he or she dangerous or just a petty criminal? |

* Some useful adjectives for your character could be: 'scared', 'careful', 'careless', 'strong', 'weak', 'mischievous', 'wayward'.

## Stage 2

| **What happens?** | Think of a problem for your character. Why is he or she in the loft? Perhaps your character is looking for something? Does something happen to make the search more difficult? |
|---|---|

## Stage 3

| **What is the ending?** | What happens to your character? Does he or she solve the problem? If yes, then how? |
|---|---|

## Stage 4

Use your plan to write your story.

- Write sentences with **detail**, using interesting **nouns** and **adjectives**. For example, instead of writing, 'The attic door shut with a bang', you could write, 'Suddenly the attic door shut with a dreadful bang and the whole house shuddered.'
- Use **connectives** to make your sentences more **varied**. For example: 'instantly', 'in front', 'behind', 'beyond', 'but', 'finally'.

### Challenge

When you have written your story, return to Stage 3 in your plan. Think of another ending for your story. Include your new ending in your story so it has **two** endings.

You will have to tell the reader about the other ending. For example you could say:

'But what if it didn't happen like that...? What if....?'

# Unit 5 Drama in the making

## 1 Two Weeks with the Queen

- Read the beginning of a play (R18)
- Learn about how plays are set out
- Develop ideas about characters and how to perform (S&L15)
- Write a short section from a play

---

**The following extract is from the opening to a play by Mary Morris, based on the novel *Two Weeks with the Queen* by Morris Gleitzman.**

*The music of* God Save the Queen *is heard, followed by the plummy voice of her Majesty delivering her Christmas message.*

*At the Mudfords' place Mum and Dad, barefoot and dressed in shorts, singlet and paper hats, are fanning themselves with a bit torn off a beer carton. They are watching*
5 *the Queen's Christmas message on TV. Colin, also in shorts and very scuffed brown elastic-sided boots, sits some way from them glaring at an open shoe box containing a pair of sensible black school shoes. His kid brother Luke runs in and out strafing everybody and everything with his new MiG fighter plane. Colin picks up a shoe and looks at it with distaste.*

| | | |
|---|---|---|
| 10 | QUEEN | And a very merry Christmas to you all. |
| | COLIN | Merry flamin' Christmas. [*Luke strafes him*] Gerroff! |
| | LUKE | Wanna go? |
| | COLIN | Get lost. |

*Luke does a circle of the room shooting down the enemy and swoops on Colin again.*
15 *Colin throws a shoe at him.*

| | | |
|---|---|---|
| | LUKE | He hit me! Dad, he hit me! |
| | DAD | Don't hit your brother, Colin. |
| | COLIN | I didn't... |
| | MUM | You heard your father. |
| 20 | COLIN | It was him, he started... |

DAD That's enough! We're trying to listen to the Queen here.

COLIN Nobody ever listens to me.

LUKE That's cos you're not the Queen.

DAD Just keep it down to a roar, eh?

25 *Dad snuggles Mum closer to him and they settle back with the Queen who rabbits on about equality and justice for all.*

COLIN [*quietly, in Luke's direction*] Lucky for you I'm not the Queen. If I was I'd have you locked in the tower and torture you and put
30 you on the rack till your bones creak and then I'd have your fingernails pulled out one by one and then I'd pour boiling oil on you and hang you from the battlements and then I'd...

LUKE Mum, I don't feel well.

COLIN Then I'd have you cut open right down the middle and your
35 guts would hang out and all the blow flies would come and the crows would peck out your eyes...

LUKE [*louder*] Mum, I feel sick.

MUM Serves you right for having four serves of chrissie pud.

COLIN Four?! I only got three!

LUKE I do, but. [*He goes back to playing with his MiG.*]

40 COLIN Prob'ly a strain of heat resistant bacteria in the chrissie pud. If I'd got a microscope for Christmas instead of a pair of school shoes I could have run some tests and spotted it. We'll prob'ly all come down with it now.

45 DAD Colin, go and shut the back door mate – keep some of the heat out.

COLIN Why can't he go?

DAD Cos I asked you to.

COLIN Yeh, well he'd be quicker, he's got turbo thrusters, I've only got
50 lace-ups.

*Mum and Dad exchange a guilty glance.*

MUM Luke, go and shut the door. [*Luke goes, Dad turns the Queen off.*] Love, about the microscope ...

DAD Next time, eh?

55 MUM We just couldn't stretch to it.

COLIN I know, the recession.

MUM Besides, you needed shoes.

COLIN [*looking at his appalling boots*] No I didn't.

DAD [*picking up a shoe*] They're pretty snazzy shoes. Bloke could end
60 up Prime Minister in shoes like those.

| | | |
|---|---|---|
| | MUM | They are the ones you liked in the shop – aren't they? |
| | COLIN | Yes, they're, um, they're good. |
| | MUM | Colin love, is there something else bothering you? |
| | COLIN | [*shrugging*] Nuh. |
| 65 | DAD | You can talk to us mate, you know that. |
| | COLIN | Well... |
| | MUM | Yes love? |
| | COLIN | It's just that... well... |
| 70 | DAD | Yes? |
| | LUKE | [*entering the room*] Mum. Mum! |
| | COLIN | Nobody ever... |

*As they turn towards Luke, he collapses on the floor. Mum and Dad rush towards him.*

| | | |
|---|---|---|
| | COLIN | Pays any attention to me. |

75 *The sound of an ambulance is heard.*

## Key Reading

### Play scripts

This text is a **play script**. Its **purpose** is to entertain the audience.

These are its main features:

- It presents a range of **characters** – their names or roles appear on the left-hand side of the page. What they say *does not* have speech marks. For example:
  DAD Don't hit your brother, Colin.
- Characters' **actions**, or how they speak, are written in the **present tense**. In this script they are presented separately from the speech, as **stage directions**. For example: *Mum and Dad exchange a guilty glance*.
- Stage directions are also used to set the scene. For example: *The music of* God Save the Queen *is heard*...

**1** In pairs, discuss the scene.

**a)** Who are the characters?

**b)** What is happening in the scene?

**2** Find an example of a **stage direction**, telling a character how to behave, or what to do. Remember, this will not be speech.

## Purpose

One of the ways the writer tries to entertain us at the start of a play is by setting up a **problem** that the characters need to overcome. We are entertained because we want to know *how* the problem will be solved.

**3** Colin obviously doesn't like the shoes he has been given for Christmas, but what is the **real problem** he is trying to explain to his parents towards the end of the scene?

The writer interests us in other ways. For example, she does not waste time introducing the problem. Even before anybody speaks, we know that Colin is not happy.

**4** Find a sentence in the **opening stage directions** that tells us Colin is unhappy.

The writer also tries to entertain us by using **humour** – by making us laugh.

**5** Find one speech by Dad that is meant to **make us laugh**.

## Reading for meaning

**6** We learn quite a lot about the sort of life the Mudford family leads in this opening scene.

**a)** **Find one speech** that tells us they do not have a lot of money.

**b)** The scene is set in Australia. Find one speech or stage direction that reminds us the family is **in Australia**. (Remember that in Australia Christmas is in the summer.)

## Focus on: Developing drama techniques

The actors who perform *Two Weeks with the Queen* need to know what their character is like. One way of doing this is by looking at what the character says.
For example, COLIN.

| What COLIN says | What this tells us about COLIN |
|---|---|
| (about the state of the house)<br>*Merry flamin' Christmas.* | a) He wants everyone to have a good Christmas.<br>b) He's not really enjoying himself. |
| (about Luke shutting the door)<br>*Why can't he go?* | c) He doesn't understand why Luke can't shut the door.<br>d) He thinks it's unfair that his parents are asking him and not Luke. |
| (about his new shoes)<br>*Yes, they're, um, good.* | e) He's trying to be polite.<br>f) He really likes his shoes. |

R18

**7** Which of the three sentences in column 2 do you think are **true**?

S&L15

**8** Now, try saying this line of Colin's in **three different ways**:
'I know, the recession.'

A **recession** is when a country's economy is in trouble, and many people can become short of money.

**a)** First, say it as if you **really understand** the problem your parents have.

**b)** Next, put stress with your voice on the word 'know', as if you are **annoyed** because you have heard all this before.

**c)** Finally, say it **sarcastically**, with the stress on 'recession', as if you think this is just an excuse for buying boring shoes instead of a microscope.

Decide which of these works best.

S&L16

**9** Read the first stage directions carefully, then look at lines 10–24. You are going to prepare this short section in groups of four.

**a)** Decide between you **who will play each part**.

**b)** Think about what you have learnt about each **character** in this unit. This should help you decide how they will say their lines and what they will do. For example:
– Colin could be rather naughty, and rude to his little brother.
– Dad could be patient and understanding.

**10** Now practise a short performance of these lines. When you are acting, make sure it is quite clear what **each character is like**.

## Key Writing

**11** The extract from Scene 2 ends with the sound of an ambulance. What do you think happens next?

- Is Luke really ill?
- Does Colin carry on trying to explain what is bothering him? Or does he keep teasing Luke?
- What happens when the ambulance arrives?
- What new character might you need?

**a)** Write eight to ten more speeches to end the scene.

**b)** Include speech from Colin and Mum or Dad.

Remember:

- to place **character names** on the left
- not to use **speech marks**
- to include **stage directions** for what characters do.

*A scene from the novel,* Two Weeks with the Queen

# How to create a stage design

- Read a set of instructions about designing a set for a play
- Explore different ways to stage a well-known story
- Learn how to work together as a group to solve problems logically (S&L13)
- Present ideas for a set design

## Creating a stage design

All plays have some sort of a stage design. Even if the design is to leave the stage blank, with no props or set, that is still a design. This is because someone has decided that is what the stage will look like. Usually this person is the Stage or Set Designer.

5 However, the Set Designer does not work alone. He or she has probably talked with the Director (the person responsible for the acting) and the Producer (the person responsible for everything else!) about the design.

So, how do you go about designing a set?

1. **Talk to the Director** to find out how he or she sees the play. For
10 example, imagine the play is a fairy-tale, like *Little Red Riding Hood*. Does the Director want a *modern* design, or a *traditional* one? Sometimes directors want modern designs so that audiences can 'relate' to the play. So, if the Director wants a modern design, perhaps tall skyscrapers would be better than tall trees.

**upstage** towards the back of the stage
**downstage** towards the front of the stage
**stage right** part of the stage on the right of an actor as they face the audience
**stage left** part of the stage on the left of an actor as they face the audience

2. **Start brainstorming ideas**. It's vital to come up with a list of possible ideas to use. After all, you don't want to suggest just one idea and then find the Director doesn't like it.
   For example:

   Little Red Riding Hood

   - Very traditional. Twisted old trees and a pretty cottage.
   - Set in a big city. Tall sky-scrapers for the forest.
   - How about a junkyard? LRRH's granny runs it?
   - Red curtains across the back of the stage, with one or two thin trees. The wolf peeps through holes in the curtains.
   - The set looks like a maze. High green hedges. LRRH is like a little princess, lost in her own garden.

3. Once you and the Director have decided on an idea, **sketch out how the stage will look** when the play starts. Of course, you may have different sets for each part of the play, but for now, stick to the opening. Do the sketch simply – there's no point in wasting time on making it too artistic.

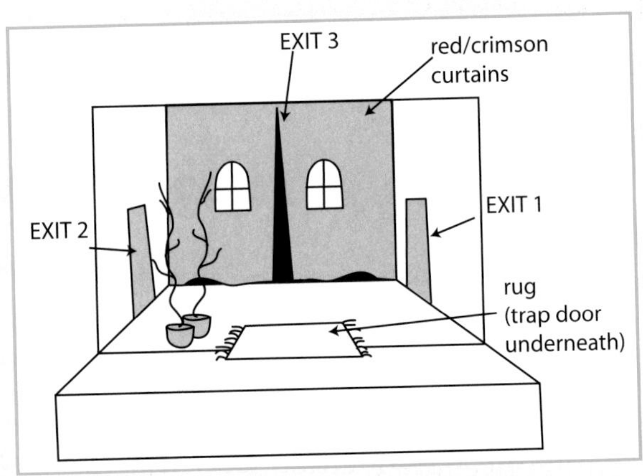


4. Once the basic design has been agreed, **write an explanation of the set** for the opening scene. You need to do this to make it clear how you see the design. This can go with the sketch, if needed.
   For example:

   ***Opening scene: Set 1***

   - The stage consists of two, dark blood-red curtains hanging down from the back of the stage (<u>upstage</u>) to suggest blood and Little Red Riding Hood's colour.
   - <u>Downstage right</u> are two thin black trees with no leaves, in order to suggest a withering, deadly place.
   - <u>Downstage centre</u> is a dusty rug, so as to cover a trap door through which the wolf enters.
   - The exits <u>stage right and left</u> consist of two wooden doors, which open outwards for practical reasons.

5. Next, think about, or **start planning**, any **scene changes** or new sets the play will need.

## Key Reading

### Instruction texts

This text is an **instruction**. Its **purpose** is to tell someone clearly how to do something. At times, this text also **explains** things to the reader.

The main features of an instruction text are:

- It has a **clear design**, with a **step-by-step** approach often supported by **pictures** or **diagrams**. For example, the diagram of the stage shows how to do a basic sketch.
- It is written in a **plain and simple** style, often using **connectives** of **time** or **sequence**. For example, '*Once* you and the Director have decided on an idea, sketch out how the stage will look *when* the play starts.'
- It uses **imperative** verbs. These are verbs that **tell** (or **command**) you to do something. For example, '*Talk* to the Director.'

S13d

**1** What do you think this text is **giving instructions about**?

**2** **Who** is the text aimed at?

**3** There are two visual aids in the text. One is the sketch of the stage. What is the other **visual aid**?

**4** Points 4 and 5 both begin with **time connectives**. What are they?

**5** There are three **imperative verbs** (command words) used in section 3. Can you find them?

## Purpose

The purpose of this text is to make the instructions clear and easy to follow. The use of numbers helps to do this.

**6** What would happen if the Set Designer **did point 3** (the sketch) ***before*** **point 2** (thinking of a range of ideas)?

**7** The first part of the text (before the numbered section) explains the job of the Set Designer. It also says that the Set Designer does not work alone. Who does he or she **usually work with**?

## Reading for meaning

**8** Why do you think someone directing or producing a play about a traditional story might decide to set it in **modern times**?

**9** In section 2, the Set Designer comes up with several different ways of staging *Little Red Riding Hood*. However, he or she doesn't just stick to the set. The Set Designer also mentions how some of the characters might be played. **Copy and complete the chart on the following page**, finding the exact reference from the text that tells you how each character might be played.

| Character | How played | Reference from text |
|---|---|---|
| Little Red Riding Hood | Little princess | 'LRRH is like a little princess, lost in her own garden.' |
| Granny | | |
| Wolf | | |
| Woodcutter | | |

**10** Make a list of things which need to be provided for the play. For example, 'blood red curtains'. Look for other **nouns** from section 4 to add to your list.

## Focus on: Working together

**Putting on any play or show at school depends on team work. This means using some special Speaking and Listening skills.**

**11** Working in small groups, imagine you have to **create a set design** for the beginning of *Two Weeks with the Queen* (see page 92). Once you have created it, you have to **present your ideas** to the class. If you are going to produce a clear, logical plan for your set design, you must work together. Here are three important things to bear in mind when you are working as a group:

- Be clear about **what** you have to do.
- Think about the **order** in which you do things.
- Think about **who** will do what.

**12** Your group has been given **two** hours to produce a design and present it to their teacher. Your task is to **plan how your group will use the two hours**.

**a)** Complete the plan using the chart below (you can add more steps).

| Steps in our plan | Time | What to do |
|---|---|---|
| Step 1 | 10 mins. | We each re-read the play on our own. |
| Step 2 | 20 mins. | We each make notes about the design. We each add a small sketch or plan. |
| Step 3 | | |
| Step 4 | | |

**b)** Once you have finished your plan, **look at it carefully**.

- Is it in a logical, sensible order?
- Is it clear who does what and for how long?

## Key Speaking and Listening

**13** Use your plan to write up your own design for the *Two Weeks with the Queen* set. You can use **notes**.

**a)** **Make notes** for your own design now. (Look at at Unit 9, which gives advice on note-making.) Include **diagrams** or **sketches** to bring your set to life. However, *don't* waste time on writing out a long description of what you want.

**b)** When you have finished, **present** your design to your group.

**c)** Decide which would be the best design to use.

Use this short checklist to make sure you support each other when presenting:

| Check | Yes | No |
|---|---|---|
| Did you get the chance to present your idea? | | |
| Did you listen to other people's ideas (without interrupting)? | | |
| Did you all agree on a final design? | | |

# 3 Reviewing Nemo

## Aims

- Read a film review
- Learn about the key features of reviews
- Speak about a film or programme you have seen (S&L19)
- Write a section from a review (S17)

**This film review about *Finding Nemo* comes from the *Unreel* website.**

**Starring: Albert Brooks, Ellen DeGeneres, Alexander Gould, Willem Dafoe, Geoffrey Rush**

The latest offering from the makers of 'Monsters Inc' and 'Toy Story' has broken box office records in the States for an animated feature film, and it is not difficult to see why, with its fantastic story, brilliant comic moments and ground-breaking visuals.

Nemo (Alexander Gould) is a young clownfish, born with lopsided fins, and the only son of Marlin (Brooks), who has recently lost his wife and unborn children in a barracuda attack. The pair live in the Great Barrier Reef, a safe existence compared to the dangers of the 'drop-off' into deep water.

Nemo's curiosity gets the better of him though, and on his first day at school he goes off into the deep, ignoring his father's warning, and ends up being captured by a scuba diver… eventually becoming an attraction in a Sydney dentist's saltwater fish tank.

Marlin, of course, is desperate to find his son, and so enlists the help of Dory (DeGeneres), a blue tang with a desperate short-term memory problem, and Bruce, a shark who is trying to become vegetarian.

20 Their mission soon becomes the stuff of legend, with everyone in the seas, and plenty more above them, seemingly aware of Marlin's strife, as he trawls the oceans for his son.

25 Nemo too has a mission: to escape from the aquarium. He also has some new found friends to help him, led by Moorish Idol fish, Gill (Dafoe).

30 They decide the time is right to take action when Nemo is chosen to be the new pet of Darla, a ghastly eight-year old, and enlist the help of Nigel the Pelican (Rush).

Pixar Studios have created another stunning film in 'Finding Nemo', proving that where they could conquer the difficulty of

35 fur in 'Monsters Inc.' they can do the same with water. They are currently producing the finest computer-animated films around, and the key to their success is plain to see. 'Finding Nemo' is an action-filled adventure, with some great comic moments, supplied in the main by Dory and Bruce, but supported by other

40 great characters such as Crush – the 150-year-old turtle with the mind and vocabulary of a teenage surfer.

It is also a touching film, with some heartwarming father/son moments. And having managed once again to bring all

45 these elements together, the end result is quite fantastic.

**clownfish** a tropical fish found on coral reefs

**lopsided** leaning to one side

**barracuda** a large and fierce fish

**enlist** persuade others to help you do something

**mission** task with a specific purpose

**trawl** search and investigate thoroughly

**elements** ingredients; the important parts of something

## Key Reading

### Reviews

This text is a **review**. Its **purpose** is to inform readers about the film, in an entertaining way.

The main features of a review are:

- It provides **key information** about the story and characters. For example, Nemo… is a young clownfish.'
- It gives us an idea of the **reviewer's opinion** of the film. This is done through the choice of words and phrases used by the reviewer. For example, 'It is also a *touching* film.' The word 'touching' suggests the film worked well because the reviewer found he was affected by it.
- It includes sentences using **noun phrases** to pack in detail. For example, '…fantastic story…great comic moments'.

**1** **What film** is being reviewed?

**2** On first reading, **what does the writer think** of the film?

**3** What do we find out about the story and characters from the review? Re-read the review and **complete these statements**:

**a)** *Nemo and his father live in…*

**b)** *But Nemo is captured by…*

**c)** *Marlin, Dory and Bruce try to…*

**4** Do we find out **how the film ends**?

**5** Find another example where the writer shows what he thinks about the film, or a part of it. Look for adjectives, such as 'a *touching* film'.

## Purpose

This review **entertains** us because when we read it, it is like seeing a mini-trailer for the film. We get small snapshots of the story and what happens.

**6** **Find one example** of a 'snapshot' from the film in paragraph 3.

We are also **informed** – not just about the story, but about what the writer thinks of Pixar Studios, who made the film. For example:

> Shows they have the skills to do things other film studios might find difficult

> Pixar Studios have created another stunning film in 'Finding Nemo', proving that where they could conquer the difficulty of fur in 'Monsters Inc.' they can do the same with water. They are currently producing the finest computer-animated films around, and the key to their success is plain to see.

**7** Which other **words or phrases** in the example on page 109 suggest that Pixar Studios are doing a good job?

## Reading for meaning

The reviewer uses the final paragraph of the review to:

- **sum up** the overall qualities of the film
- **praise** Pixar Studios, the makers of the film.

The summary mentions that the film:

- is an 'action-packed adventure'
- has some 'great comic moments'.

**8** Is the film 'action-packed'? Does it have 'comic moments'? Find **two examples** of exciting events or comic moments from the review.

## Focus on: Evaluating spoken presentations

As you have seen, a good review includes **information** and the reviewer's **opinion** (what he or she thinks about the film).

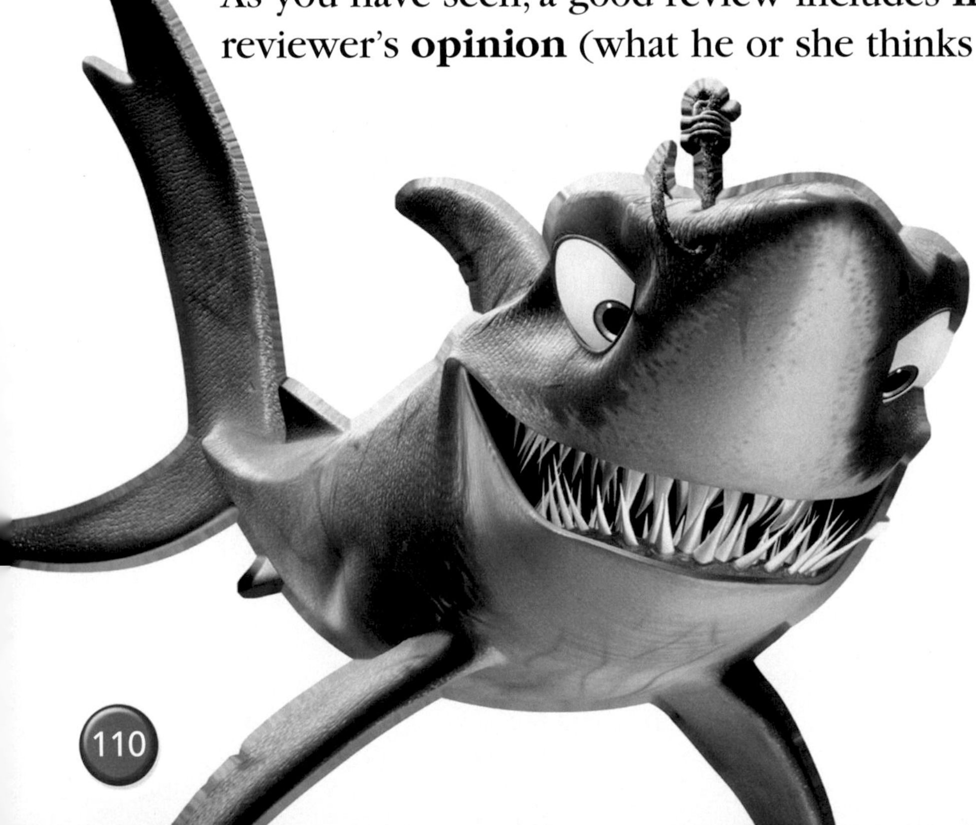

## Grammar for reading

A **noun** is a word that names something. Often a group of words does the same job, for example, 'The deep-sea divers'. This is called a **noun phrase**.

The reviewer has to pack in a lot of information into one phrase or sentence, so often uses noun phrases.

…fantastic story…

This noun tells us exactly which bit the reviewer is focusing on – the plot (what happens)

This adjective tells us what the reviewer thinks

S&L19

**9** Imagine you have been asked to review a **film** or **television programme** you have seen recently.

**a)** **Describe the plot** of the film or TV programme to a partner. Use phrases like the one above about *Finding Nemo*.

- Some words you could use are: 'fantastic', 'amazing', 'funny', 'stupid', 'complicated'.
- Add as much of your own detail as you want.

**b)** Now say something about the **main character**, using the noun phrases from the chart below or making up your own. For example, 'It's about this…'

| **Adjective** | **Noun** |
|---|---|
| muscular | waitress |
| beautiful | detective |
| lonely | footballer |
| shy | child |
| quiet | secret agent |

**c)** Now say **what you like** about this film or programme.
For example:

> 'Well, it had a different ending/funny opening scene…'
> 'I liked the main character because…'

**10** After you have finished, ask your friend **how well** you reviewed the programme or film. Did you:

- Give some **basic information** about the story and people in it?
- Use **noun phrases** in your descriptions?
- Give **your opinion** at the end?

## Key Writing

S17 **11** Write the **summary paragraph** of your film or programme review. You should:

- Summarise the film or programme, giving some **information** about the story ('great comic moments') or characters, and also stating **what you think**.
- Try to use **noun phrases** like the ones you have practised in your spoken description.

Use this writing frame to help you:

| | |
|---|---|
| Say something about the story or characters. | *[Name of film/TV programme]* has some…<br>and… |
| Finish with a statement about the programme or film and what you think of it. | It is a...film/programme…<br>and… |

# 4 Unit 5 Assignment: TV reviewer

## Assessment Focuses

- AF7 Select appropriate and effective vocabulary

**You:** write reviews of television programmes for a national magazine called *Top TV*. It lists the programmes for all channels and has reviews (or previews) of the week's programmes.

**Your task:** to write a review of an upcoming episode of the soap opera *EastEnders*.

## Stage 1

You have watched the episode. Read through the notes you made.

**Where:** *Set in Walford, East London. Mostly based around Albert Square. Various other locations, including Bridge Street market.*

**Who:** *The Fowlers: mother Pauline, son Martin and Martin's wife Sonya. They own a fruit stall on Bridge Street market.*

*The Beales: father Ian, children Lucy, Peter and Bobby. Ian owns the chip shop and café.*

*The Moons: Alfie, his wife Kat, his brother Spencer and their grandmother Nana Moon. They run the Queen Vic pub.*

***Other characters:***

*Dot Branning: long time resident of Walford. Works at the laundrette and is best friends with Pauline Fowler.*

*Lynne and Garry Hobbes: Kat Moon's sister and her husband. They are expecting their first child.*

***Main storyline:*** *Fairground ride collapses during Bridge Street fair – many people injured. Pregnant Lynne is rushed to hospital. Ian is hurt beneath rubble but worries about Peter and Lucy's safety. Dot and Pauline are trapped together, they argue. Spencer's leg is mangled; Kat comforts him. She finds out Alfie has left Walford, but when he hears of the disaster he races back to the Square!*

## Stage 2

Decide what **opinion** you have of the episode – was it good or bad? Now write down at least **five key adjectives** you might use in your review. Some examples are provided in the chart below.

| Good | Bad |
|---|---|
| believable | unbelievable |
| interesting | boring |
| moving | cold (as in 'leaving you cold') |
| watchable | unwatchable |
| exciting | unexciting |
| pacy | slow |
| clever | silly, stupid |
| funny | unfunny |
| dramatic | dull |

## Stage 3

Now write **three descriptions** of main characters, using the adjective + noun structure (see page 111 for help). For example:

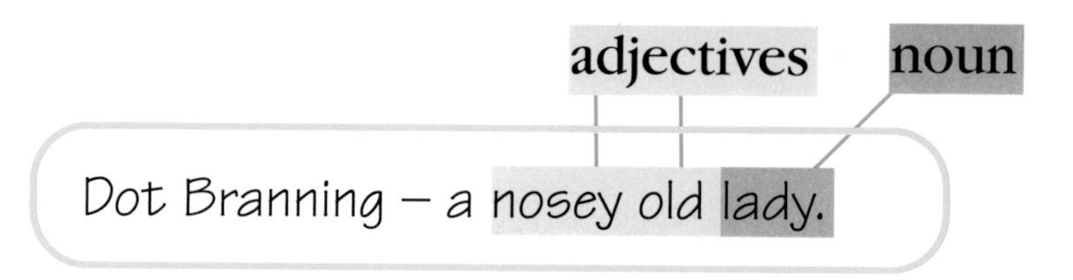


## Stage 4

Now **draft your review**. Use the following plan to help you:

| | |
|---|---|
| **Paragraph 1:** Introduce the programme and set the scene. | *Tonight, another episode of EastEnders hits our screens. The action takes place at the Bridge Street fair…* |
| **Paragraph 2:** Write about the main storyline, including descriptions of the main characters. | *In this episode we learn that a fairground ride has collapsed and Dot Cotton, a nosey old lady, has been trapped…* |
| **Final paragraph:** Write about your opinion of the episode. | *EastEnders is…* |

### Challenge

Try writing an **alternative** last paragraph. In it, take the **opposite** point of view. For example, if you said you liked the episode in your first review, write about hating it in your second review.

# Unit 6 Far from home

## 1 If a snake bites...

### Aims

- Read a text telling you how to deal with a snake bite
- Explore how instructions are written (S13d)
- Think about how to compare the way people do things (W18)
- Give a set of simple instructions to guide a plane (S&L4)

**The following text comes from a leaflet. The leaflet is aimed at children visiting Australia.**

# What to do for snake bites

If a snake bites you or your friend,
then you will need to know what to do.

## Be prepared

- Make sure that you carry a roll of **crepe bandage** with you when you go for a walk through the bush or long grass. 5
- Taking a **mobile phone** can also be very useful, as you can call for help if you need it. 10

## First aid

- Do not wash the bite area. If there is some venom on the skin, this can help doctors find out which snake caused the bite, so they can give some anti-venom to help fight
15 the snake poison.
- Wrap a bandage firmly around the place where the bite is. (This should not be so tight that the blood supply is cut off. If the bandage hurts, it is too tight.)
- If the bite is on an arm or leg, wrap another bandage over
20 as much of the limb as possible.
- Stop the person from using the arm or leg by putting on a splint (this can be a long stick).
- **Keep the injured person still.**
- Try to keep the person calm. Poison spreads more quickly
25 if the heart beats faster.

## Some things not to do

- Do not wait to see if the bite causes any problems. Always treat it straight away.
30 - Do not cut, wash or suck the bite. (Ignore all those old cowboy movies where the hero sucked out the poison!)
- Do not use ice on the bite. It will not be helpful.

35
## Take action

- **Get help**. The faster the better.
- If there are at least two other people, you could try to carry the person to where help is, but don't make the bitten
40 person walk.

**crepe** light cotton fabric
**venom** poison
**anti-venom** something to fight the poison

## Key Reading

### Instruction texts

This text is an **instruction.** Its **purpose** is to tell someone clearly how to do something.

The main features of an instruction text are:

- It has a **clear design**, with a **step-by-step** approach often supported by **pictures** or **diagrams**. For example, the bullet points show where each instruction begins.
- It uses **imperative** verbs. These are verbs that tell (or **command**) you to do something. For example, '*Get* help'.
- It is written in a **plain and simple** style. You need to be able to understand the instructions and follow them easily. For example, 'Try to keep the person calm.'

1 The instructions in this leaflet have been arranged in four sections. The first is 'Be prepared'. What are the other sections?

2 Imperative verbs address the reader directly. Find **two more examples** from the leaflet.

3 One way of using a plain and simple style is to make your sentences short. Find **three short sentences** in the leaflet.

## Purpose

The purpose of this text is to tell you what to do if you or your friend gets bitten by a snake. Obviously, it is very important that you act quickly. So the instructions must also get to the point quickly.

One way the writer does this is to use **imperatives**. It helps even more if the imperative is put at the front of the sentence:

'Wrap a bandage firmly around the place where the bite is.'

This is much more effective than a general statement, such as:

'It is a good idea to wrap a bandage firmly …'

**4** Read the following sentences with a partner, and **reword them** so that they become short, snappy instructions. The first one has been done for you:

- Sun-tan cream offers protection from the sun for a short time, but you must keep putting it on. For example, 'Keep putting on the sun-tan cream. It only offers protection for a short time.'
- If you don't want to be burnt, you shouldn't stay out in the sun for long periods.
- Extra care is needed when you visit hot countries like Australia.

## Reading for meaning

**5** Sometimes reasons are given for the instructions, for example, 'Taking a mobile phone can also be very useful, *as you can call for help if you need it.*' Find **one other place** where a reason is given.

**6** The writer has printed some phrases and sentences in red. What **effect** does this have?

**7** Instruction texts are generally written in the present tense. For example, 'If the bite *is* on an arm or leg…'. Find **three more verbs** written in the present tense.

**8** Look at the section headed 'Some things not to do'.

**a)** How has the writer organised this section so that it is easy to see where a new instruction starts?

**b)** Each instruction consists of two sentences. Which is the **most important sentence** in each case?

## Focus on: Comparative adverbs

**Adverbs** are used with verbs to describe *how* you do something. They often end with the letters *-ly*. For example, 'He speaks *quickly*.'

Sometimes you need to compare two ways of doing something. You can then use a **comparative adverb**.

Look at these sentences:

Poison spreads quickly.

Simple adverb describes how the poison spreads

Poison spreads more quickly if the heart beats faster.

Comparative adverb compares how quickly the poison spreads when the heart beats faster with how quickly it spreads normally

To make a comparative adverb, you add the word 'more' in front of it.

W18

**9** a) **Copy out and underline** the adverb in the following sentences:

- Jack spoke quietly.
- Karen crossed the road carefully.
- The car runs smoothly.

b) Then **rewrite each sentence** using a comparative adverb. Use the clauses provided below to help you compare the action with something else. You will create a longer sentence, as in the example above.

- than his brother Zack
- when it was rush hour
- if I check the oil every month

# Key Speaking and Listening

S&L4 **10** In groups of three, you are going to work on **giving spoken instructions**.

- One of you is an **air traffic controller**. Your task is to give clear spoken instructions to the pilot, as the plane's computer has failed.
- One of you is an **air pilot**. You do exactly what you are told by the air traffic controller.
- One of you is an **observer**. You must point out when the pilot is not following the instructions exactly. You can also suggest how the air traffic controller can improve their instructions.

You will each have a turn as the air traffic controller. Your job is to **guide the pilot** to a destination you have chosen, or which your teacher has given you, using the map below and without naming any country.

For example: Travel east for 200 miles.
Slow down as we are close to the destination.

# 2 Discovering Brazil

- Read two information texts on Brazil
- Explore how information texts are written (S13a)
- Think about the effect of putting nouns at the beginning of your sentences
- Compare and contrast the way information is presented (R3)
- Rewrite an information text in a different way

---

**Both of the following texts give you information about Brazil. Text 1 is from a website. Text 2 is an extract from a children's encyclopaedia.**

## Text 1

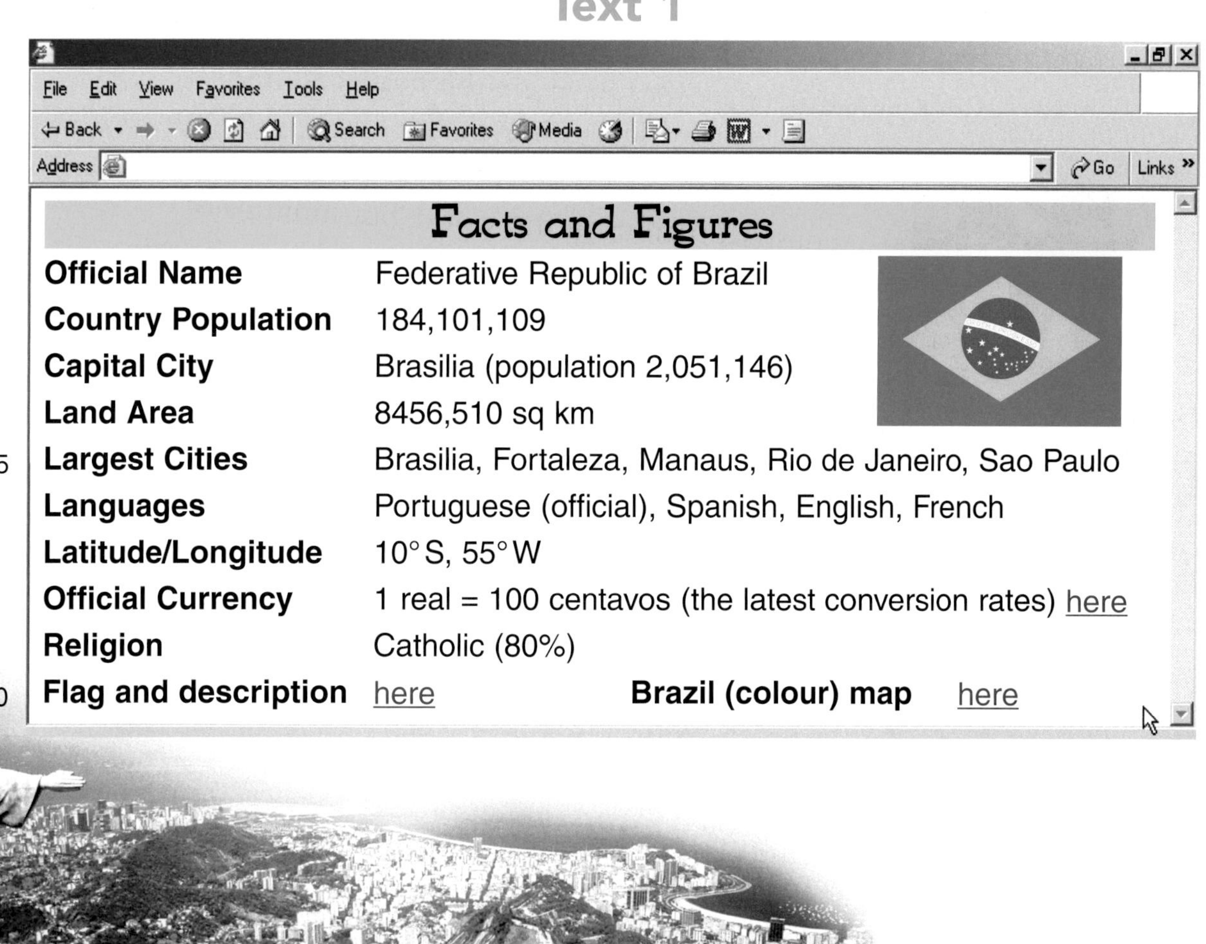

File Edit View Favorites Tools Help

Back Search Favorites Media

Address Go Links

### Facts and Figures

| | |
|---|---|
| **Official Name** | Federative Republic of Brazil |
| **Country Population** | 184,101,109 |
| **Capital City** | Brasilia (population 2,051,146) |
| **Land Area** | 8456,510 sq km |
| **Largest Cities** | Brasilia, Fortaleza, Manaus, Rio de Janeiro, Sao Paulo |
| **Languages** | Portuguese (official), Spanish, English, French |
| **Latitude/Longitude** | 10° S, 55° W |
| **Official Currency** | 1 real = 100 centavos (the latest conversion rates) here |
| **Religion** | Catholic (80%) |
| **Flag and description** | here **Brazil (colour) map** here |

Text 2

# Brazil

Brazil is the largest country in South America. This huge territory covers nearly half the continent; it is almost as big as the USA. In the west are the foothills of the massive Andes mountains. To the east lie the beautiful beaches on the coast of the vast Atlantic ocean. However, even though it is a large country, a lot of Brazil is hard to access. The north-eastern corner of the country is dry and made up mostly of thorny scrub. The Amazon basin also has a very small population. Most Brazilians live in the cities – the three biggest cities are Sao Paolo, Brasilia (the capital) and beautiful Rio de Janiero. Rio is famous for its colourful annual carnival. Brazilians are a vibrant mixture of races and cultures and this is reflected in their music, dance and art.

Brazil is one of the biggest producers of coffee in the world. Another important export is citrus fruit. Cattle, pigs and sheep are the most common livestock and there are also large deposits of iron ore and other minerals. Brazil is one of the ten biggest industrial nations in the world, but millions of people are poor, while only a few are very wealthy.

The national sport in Brazil is football (or *futebol* as Brazilians call it). They are the only nation to have won the World Cup four times (1958, 1962, 1970 and 1994) and are known to play the most creative and exciting style of the game. Brazilians are passionate about football – it is played all year round, and on big international game days, no one goes to work. Brazil's most famous player is Pelé, who retired in 1977. He scored over 1,000 goals in his 22-year career, and is known in Brazil as O Rei (the king).

**scrub** dry area of stunted trees and bushes

**iron ore** iron in its natural form in the ground

**minerals** inorganic substances found in the ground, for example, metals and salts.

## Key Reading

### Information texts

These texts are **information** texts. Their **purpose** is to present information on a subject in a clear way.

The main features of information texts are:

- They have **clear organisation**. The information is arranged in paragraphs or separate sections. For example, the third paragraph of Text 2 is about football.
- Verbs are in the **present tense**. Information texts describe how things *are*. For example, in Text 2 it says: 'Brazil *is* the largest country in South America'.
- They use **factual writing**. The language is clear and precise. Technical terms or specialist words are often used. For example, in Text 2 it says: '...there are also large *deposits of iron ore and other minerals*.'

**1** Find one way in which the information in Text 1 is **presented** or **organised clearly**. Then find one example in Text 2.

**2** Add a **verb** to one of the lines in Text 1, so that it makes a sentence. What tense is your verb?

**3** Text 2 contains some **technical terms** that are used in geography. Find the words or phrases in the text that are nearest in meaning to the following:

**a)** the lowest slope of a mountain

**b)** the things that are sold to other countries

**c)** a layer of ore or minerals.

## Purpose

The purpose of an information text is to **describe the way things are**. Most texts do this in a clear and straightforward way. This is so that the reader (a) can find the information they want quickly, and (b) understand it easily.

Often **nouns** are used to begin sentences. This is so that the reader knows exactly what the sentence is going to be about. For example, in lines 12–13 of Text 2 this sentence appears:

> Rio is famous for its colourful annual carnival.

The **noun** 'Rio' tells you what this sentence is going to be about

In line 1 a **noun phrase** does the same job.

The **noun phrase** 'this huge territory' tells you this sentence is going to be about Brazil

This huge territory covers nearly half the continent; it is almost as big as the USA.

The **pronoun** 'it' refers to Brazil. It tells you that the next part of the sentence is still about the country

**4** Look at the last two sentences of Text 2. **What are they about**? How has the writer made this clear? Use the terms **noun** and **noun phrase** in your answer.

### Grammar for reading

A **noun** is a word that names something. Often a group of words does the same job, for example, 'The deep-sea divers'. This is called a **noun phrase**.

A **pronoun** is a word used to replace a noun or a noun phrase, e.g. 'it', 'she', 'he', 'them', 'its', 'hers', 'his', 'their'.

## Reading for meaning

**5** Answer these questions about **football in Brazil**. You will find the answers in lines 23–36 of Text 2:

**a)** Find the Brazilian word for football.

**b)** In which years did Brazil win the World Cup?

**c)** Who is the most famous Brazilian footballer?

**6** How does the writer **organise his material** to give the reader a 'tour' of the country in lines 1–15? Look closely at sentences 3 and 4.

**7** In pairs, **invent a quiz** on Brazil for your partner. One of you writes down three questions based on Text 1. The other writes down three questions based on Text 2. Take it in turns to read out the questions, one at a time. When you give the answer, back it up by pointing to the evidence in the text. For example:

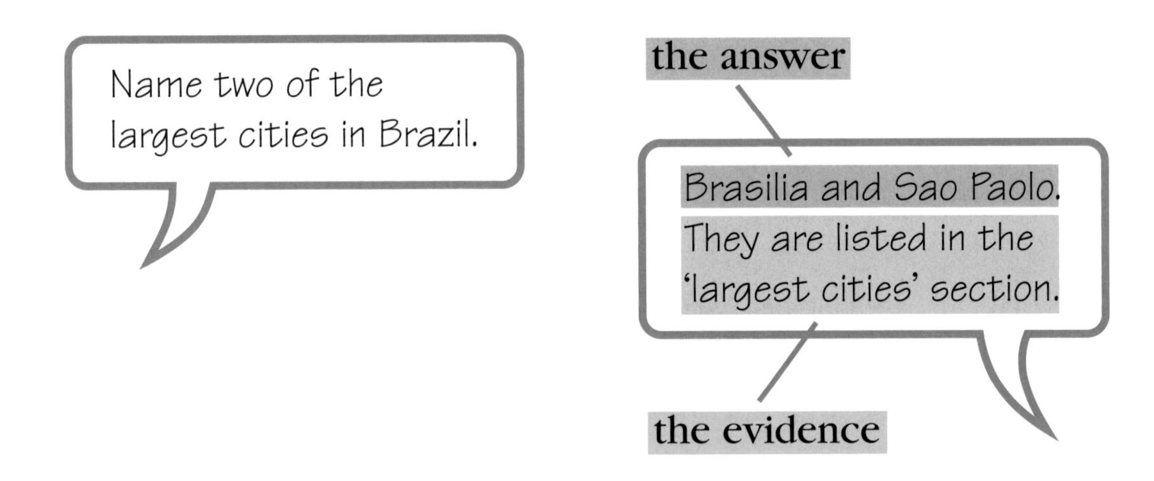


## Focus on: Presenting the information



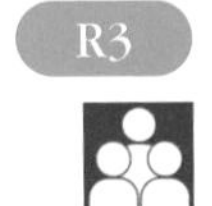

**Information can be presented in many different ways, depending on the exact purpose of the text.**

**8** In groups, **compare and contrast** the two information texts on Brazil. **Draw up a table** like the one on page 129, and complete it.

| | Web page | Encyclopaedia entry |
|---|---|---|
| **Design/layout**<br>Comments on… | | |
| Use of bold/italic and colour | Bold used to show the subheadings – simple but clear. Colour to mark the main heading, and the hyperlinks – makes them stand out | Bold used for title only. Could do with some more bold to highlight main words? |
| The size and style of the type face | | |
| The illustrations | | |
| Headings and subheadings | | |
| **Language and style**<br>Comments on… | | |
| Length of sentences | | |
| Use of paragraphs | No paragraphs, as text is made up of notes | 3 paragraphs, because dealing with 3 topics. This helps the reader follow the text. |

**9** Finally, think about the exact purpose of each text. Does this explain the differences in the table?
Be prepared to present your table to the class.

## Key Writing

**10** Your task is to present the information in paragraphs 1 and 2 of Text 2 so that it looks like a **fact file**. In this fact file, there are headings and notes but no sentences (just like Text 1).
You could begin like this:

**Brazil**

*Where is it?*
- South America

*Geography*
- Dry in north-east

*Size*
- Largest country in South America
- Almost size of the USA

# 3 Bournemouth in the rain

## Aims

- Read a traveller's tale about a rainy visit (R6)
- Explore how recount texts are written and structured (S13b)
- Analyse how paragraphs are used to mark a change of focus (S8)
- Imagine how the tale continued, and write the next episode

**The American writer Bill Bryson lived in Britain from 1973 to 1995. This is an extract from his account of a trip he took before he left.**

## Bournemouth in the rain

And so to Bournemouth. I arrived at five-thirty in the evening in a driving rain. Night had fallen heavily and the streets were full of swishing cars, their headlights sweeping through bullets of shiny rain. I'd lived in Bournemouth for two years and thought I knew it reasonably well, but the area around the station had been extensively rebuilt, with new roads and office blocks and one of those befuddling networks of pedestrian subways that force you to surface every few minutes like a gopher to see where you are.

By the time I reached the East Cliff, a neighbourhood of medium-sized hotels perched high above a black sea, I was soaked through and muttering. The one thing to be said for Bournemouth is that you are certainly spoiled for choice with hotels. Among the many gleaming palaces of comfort that lined every street for

blocks around, I selected an establishment on a side-street for no reason other than I rather liked its sign: neat capitals in pink neon glowing through the slicing
20 rain. I stepped inside, shedding water, and could see at a glance it was a good choice – clean, nicely old-fashioned, attractively priced, and with the kind of warmth that makes your glasses steam and brings on sneezing fits. I decanted several ounces of water from
25 my sleeve and asked for a single room for two nights.

'Is it raining out?' the reception girl asked brightly as I filled in the registration card between sneezes and pauses to wipe water from my face with the back of my arm.

'No, my ship sank and I had to swim the last seven
30 miles.'

'Oh, yes?' she went on in a manner that made me suspect she was not attending to my words closely. 'And will you be dining with us tonight, Mr –' she glanced at my water-smeared card ' – Mr Brylcreem?' I
35 considered the alternative – a long slog through stair-rods of rain – and felt inclined to stay in. Besides, between her cheerily bean-sized brain and my smeared scrawl, there was every chance they would charge the meal to another room. I said I'd eat in, accepted a key
40 and drippingly found my way to my room.

**befuddling** confusing

**gopher** small North American creature which lives partly underground

**blocks** areas of land with streets on their sides

**decanted** poured out

**considered** thought about

**felt inclined to** preferred

## Key Reading

### Recount texts

This text is a **recount**. Its **purpose** is to recount or tell the reader about a series of events.

The main features of a recount text are:

- It is mainly told in the **past tense**. For example, 'I *arrived* at five-thirty in the evening...'
- It describes events in **time order** and uses **connectives of time**. For example, '*By the time* I reached the East Cliff...'
- It uses **paragraphs** to mark a change of focus. For example, 'And so to Bournemouth.'

**1** There are **six verbs** in the **past tense** in the first five lines of this passage. Work with a partner to identify them all.

**2** Put these actions in the **correct time order** (they are all in the second paragraph):

**a)** 'I asked for a single room for two nights'

**b)** 'I stepped inside, shedding water'

**c)** 'I decanted several ounces of water from my sleeve'

**d)** 'I could see at a glance it was a good choice'

How do you know they are in the right order?

**3** Where in the extract does Bryson **change his focus** from Bournemouth as a whole to just one part of Bournemouth? How does he signal this to the reader?

## Purpose

**Some texts do more than simply recount events in a factual way. They also aim to entertain the reader.**

**4** 'Bournemouth in the rain' has three extra ingredients, which make it an **entertaining** recount:

- good descriptions
- dialogue
- humour

**a)** Read the **description** of pedestrian subways in paragraph 1. Discuss with a partner what makes it effective.

**b)** In the second half of the passage, which bit of **dialogue** belongs to Bill Bryson? How do you know?

**c)** Which is **funnier** – the description of the subway in paragraph 1 or the passage of dialogue? Be prepared to give your reasons.

**dialogue** a conversation between two people. This can be spoken or written down.

## Reading for meaning

**A good way of getting to grips with what is actually happening in a recount text is to ask yourself the five 'W' questions:**

- **who**
- **what**
- **where**
- **when**
- **why**

R6

**5** Read the extract again carefully, and discuss these questions with a partner:

a) **Who** is this recount about?

b) **What** does this person do?

c) **Where** is it set?

d) **When** did it happen?

e) **Why** did Bill Bryson decide to 'eat in'?

**6** There are lots of references to rain, water and wetness in this passage. You could say that it almost drips off the page!

a) Write down **six words or phrases** that refer to the rain.

b) Highlight the **verbs**, **nouns** and **adjectives** in three different colours on your list.

c) Which is the **best word or phrase**, in your opinion?

**7** How do you think the **extract continues**? Imagine that Bill Bryson has 'drippingly' found his room. What happens next? **Discuss a few ideas** with a partner, choose the best one and jot down a few **notes** for it.

## Focus on: Structuring a recount text

A recount text describes a series of events. These events can be plotted on a **timeline**. A timeline is also a good tool for planning your own recounts.

S13b

**8** A timeline for *Bournemouth in the rain* has been started below. **Copy it out and complete it**. Only include the most important events.

I arrived at Bournemouth, 5.30pm

I reached the East Cliff

S8

**9** A paragraph is a group of sentences that are all about the same topic. If an event in a recount deals with a different person, place or idea, it usually begins a new paragraph. Look back at the text.

**a)** What different **focus** has the writer given to each paragraph?

**b)** Find the **words or phrase** that signals each paragraph focus.

For example, the focus of paragraph 1 is the town centre of Bournemouth. 'And so to Bournemouth' signals this.

## Key Writing

**10** Earlier you imagined what happened when Bill Bryson got to his bedroom. Your task now is to **write two or three short paragraphs** describing this.

**a)** First of all, draw a **timeline** of events.

**b)** Then think about how you are going to organise your material into **paragraphs**.

**c)** Finally, **write** your recount.

Remember:

- Imagine that you are Bill Bryson. Use 'I' and 'my' (the **first person**).
- Describe events as if they happened in the past. Put the events in **time order** and use the **past tense**.
- Make your recount **entertaining**. Include good descriptions, dialogue and/or humour.

# Unit 6 Assignment: Travel guide to Greece

## Assessment Focuses

- AF3 Organise and present whole texts effectively, sequencing and structuring information, ideas and events
- AF4 Construct paragraphs and use cohesion within and between paragraphs

**You:** are a travel writer.
**Your task:** to write a short factual introduction for a travel guide to Greece.

## Stage 1

Here is some information about Greece. It is written in note form. As you can see, it has been organised into three topics. The topic names are given below. Your first task is to work out **which set** of **notes belongs with which topic**.

| General information | Tourist attractions | Natural features |
|---|---|---|

**A**
- mostly mainland
- over 1400 islands
- main islands: Crete Euboea, Rhodes, Chios, Corfu
- nearly 80% of country is mountains/hills

**B**
- official name: Hellenic Republic
- location: in south-east Europe, on the Mediterranean Sea
- area: 132,000 sq km
- capital: Athens
- currency: euro

**C**
- climate: hot dry summers
- seaside: lots of beaches and islands
- ancient sites and cities like Knossos
- character: relaxed, child-friendly

## Stage 2

You are going to write **one paragraph on each topic**. First of all, decide which **order** you want the paragraphs to go in. Remember that the most important, or the most general, information goes first.

## Stage 3

Finally, turn these notes into **three clear paragraphs** for your introduction to Greece.

Remember:

- Use the **present tense**. You are describing how Greece is now.
- This is **factual writing**. Your sentences must be clear and precise.
- It is especially important to tell your reader what each paragraph is about. Signal the **focus of new paragraphs** clearly.

You may like to begin like this:

**Greece**

Greece is a country in south-east Europe, on the Mediterranean Sea.
Its official name is the Hellenic Republic.

# Unit 7 Media today

## 1 Words and pictures

- Look at two adverts and explore how they persuade the reader (S13e)
- Explore the importance of images and design in adverts (R11)
- Analyse the ways that words can be persuasive in adverts (S&L8)
- Defend a point of view in a persuasive way (S&L5)

**Look at the adverts on the following two pages. The first is for Wall's Carte D'Or ice cream.**

**crema di mascarpone** cream made with mascarpone (an Italian cream cheese)
**pistachio** a type of nut

**The following advert appears in a tourist brochure for Blackpool.**

**league** an old-fashioned unit of distance (about 3 miles). Jules Verne wrote a famous adventure story called *20,000 Leagues Under the Sea*

## Key Reading

### Persuasion texts

These are **persuasion** texts. Their **purpose** is to persuade the reader to do something.

The main features of persuasion texts are:

- They include a **series of points**, in a **logical order**, supporting a single viewpoint, for example, 'Blackpool Sea Life Centre...is a watery world of all things marine.'
- They use **visual images** or **sound** to grab the interest of the audience, for example, the main image in the ice cream advert.
- They use **colourful** and **suggestive** language, for example, '...sh-sh-shudder as sharks pass within inches'.

**1** The advert for the Sea Life Centre makes lots of points. Find **two important points** that it makes.

**2** How much of the Wall's advert is **picture**? How much is **text**? Is one more important than the other?

**3** The Sea Life Centre uses the slogan '20,000 leagues ahead of the rest!' How effective is this slogan?

**suggestive** suggesting a particular meaning or image

**slogan** an easily-remembered phrase used to sell a product

### Purpose

**4** Look at the Wall's advert. What is its **main purpose**:

- to get you to buy Wall's *Crema di Mascarpone* ice cream
- to give you information about Wall's *Crema di Mascarpone* ice cream?

**5** Look at the Sea Life Centre advert. What is its **main purpose**:

- to get you to visit the Sea Life Centre
- to advertise a new film, 'Voyage to the Bottom of the Sea'?

## Reading for meaning

'Reading' an advert means far more than looking at the words. The design of the advert is very important too – especially its pictures.

Look at what we can say about the design of the Wall's advert:

**colour scheme:**
- bold colours
- mostly red and white, but green of nuts also used
- colours of design match colours of ice cream

**main text:**
- large clear capitals
- takes up top third of page
- shaped around the image

**main image:**
- large and clear
- in centre of page
- set at an angle
- shows product name on side

**logo:**
- tucked out of the way
- but not hidden: it pushes into picture area

R11

**6** In pairs, look at the Sea Life Centre advert. Discuss **how effective the design is**. Talk about:

- the pictures used (for example, subjects, colours, shapes, number)
- how the text is presented (for example, size, colour, variety).

## Focus on: Colourful and suggestive words

Sometimes there are very few words in an advert. But every word will be carefully chosen to persuade you to buy something or do something.

There are many ways in which the words can be persuasive:

- They can address the reader directly, for example, using 'you' or commands.
- They can be colourful or powerful, for example, lively adjectives, or words that make a particular sound.
- They can be emotive or suggestive, for example, they make you feel something, or they suggest a particular image or meaning.

Look at how the words in the Wall's advert persuade you in all of these ways:

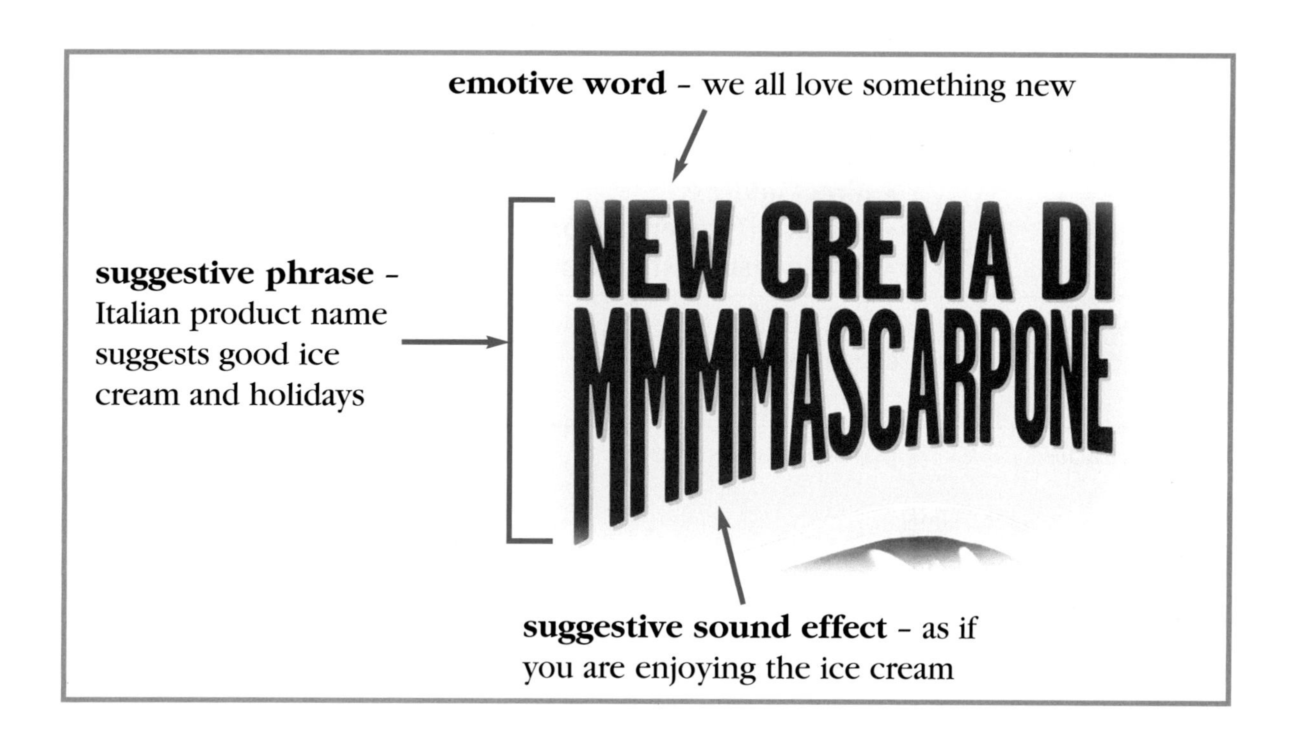


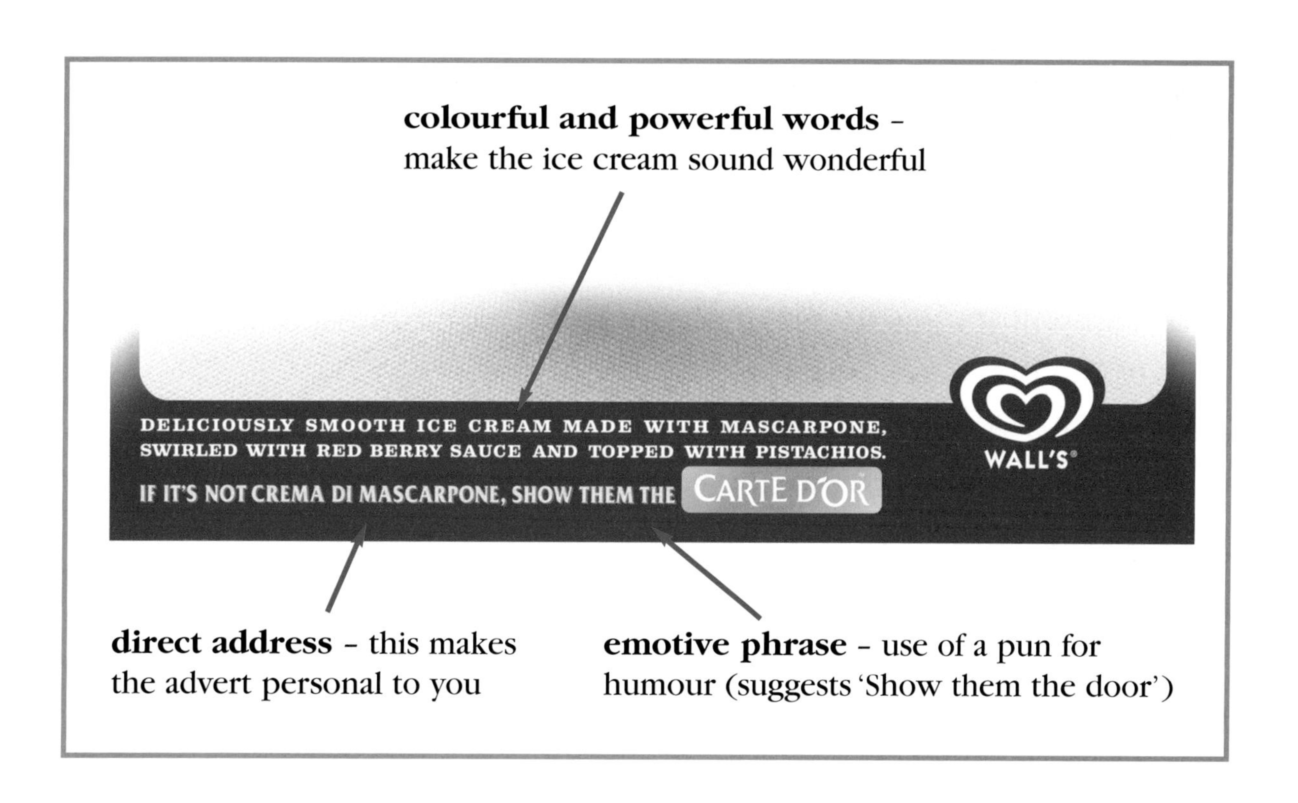

S&L8

**7** In groups, talk about the way words are used persuasively in the panel at the top left of the Sea Life Centre advert. Then **draw up a chart** like the one below to record your findings.

| **Word/phrase** | **Type of persuasion used:**<br>• **direct address**<br>• **colourful/powerful words**<br>• **emotive/suggestive words** | **What effect it has** |
|---|---|---|
| All aboard | direct address<br>suggestive phrase | Grabs reader from the start. The phrase also suggests you are about to go on a voyage. |
| unforgettable | powerful adjective | Makes reader feel it will be a great experience. |

## Key Speaking and Listening

S&L5

**8** In the same groups, your task is to **defend one of these points of view**:

- The Sea Life Centre is an effective advert.
- The Sea Life Centre is not an effective advert.

You will do this by presenting your work on questions 6 and 7 to the class. You will need to:

- Give **reasons** or **evidence** for your statements. For example, 'The colours of the advert are *effective because they remind you of the sea.*'
- Speak in a **persuasive** way, using direct address and powerful words. For example, 'Don't you think the colours are just fantastic?'

Practise your presentation in groups.

#  The power of advertising

## Aims

- Read a newspaper article that expresses a point of view about advertising
- Explore how argument texts are written (S13e)
- Think about how sentences are organised into paragraphs (S10)

**The following text is a column from *The Independent*. In the column, Lisa Markwell describes how even her young son, Peter, is affected by the power of advertising.**

## The advertising is working, damn it

Why is it that my son knows how much the latest Teenage Mutant Ninja Turtles playset costs, but doesn't know six times seven? Why does he suggest that we (5) have Wall's sausage balls for supper, but can't remember what he had for lunch? It is, of course, the power of advertising. He only watches television for about one (10) hour on Saturday morning, and one afternoon a week. But in those brief moments, he's wide-eyed (and wide-brained) to soak up the messages directed at him. (15)

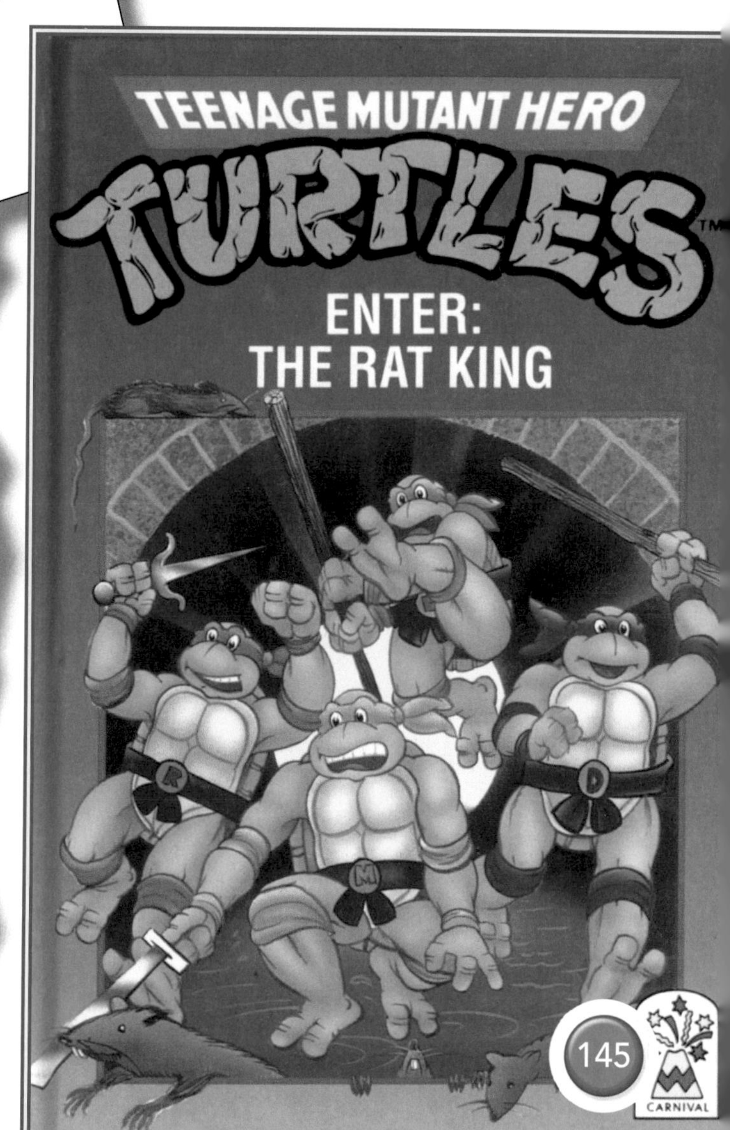

New research by Harris Interactive shows that seven-year-olds are old enough to be a target consumer for youth market advertising. The idea is, apparently, get 'em young and then when they're old enough to spend, they will be indoctrinated in the delights of, well, probably Sunny Delight.

What used to be an advertising frenzy in the weeks before Christmas doesn't seem to be abating as summer approaches. My son doesn't actually have any money to spend on junk food, plastic toys and identikit pop – he gets very little pocket money and is a careful saver. But that doesn't stop him remembering the consumer goodies.

Peter and his class mates also spend a great deal of time poring over the Argos catalogue. Every Bionicle figure is noted; every Barbie accessory is studied. If only they took as much notice of their times tables.

But if I'm honest, I would have to say that their retail interest is a product of our times. We are all consumers now, whether of penny sweets or second homes. Last week, while on holiday, Peter sang the jingle for Kandoo lavatory wipes (the soundtrack to daring himself deeper into the sea – 'you can do it with Kandoo'). Then there was 'I shall eat a fishy on a little dishy' as we walked to a restaurant on the harbour.

But what really worried me was when he said: 'Mum, did you know that calls with Tele2 are only 2p, that's cheaper than BT?' No I didn't and I want to know more. The advertising is working, damn it.

**indoctrinated** taught, brainwashed
**abating** dying down
**frenzy** wild excitement
**retail interest** interest in buying things
**product of our times** part of modern life

# Key Reading

## Argument texts

This is an **argument** text. Its **purpose** is to express a point of view, and persuade the reader to agree with it.

The main features of an argument text are:

- It includes a **series of points**, in a **logical order**. For example, the fourth paragraph makes a point about the Argos catalogue.
- The points are backed up by **evidence** or **reasons**. For example, 'New research by Harris Interactive shows…'
- It uses mostly **formal** but **effective** language. For example, 'Every Bionicle figure is noted; every Barbie accessory is studied.'

**1** The main point the author makes in the first paragraph is that advertising is powerful. What **new point** does she make in paragraph 2?

**2** What exactly does the **evidence** of the Harris research show (paragraph 2)?

**3** The phrase 'advertising frenzy' in paragraph 3 is an **effective** one. What picture does this create?

## Purpose

The purpose of an argument text is to win the audience over to your point of view. What is this writer's **point of view**? What is the main point she is making?

The author wins the audience over to her view by **backing up her points**. There are three main ways that she does this:

- by giving **evidence** or **reasons** for her view
- by referring to her **own experience**
- by giving an **example** of what she is saying (i.e. change perspective).

**4** The writer's view is that advertising is powerful. What **evidence** is given in paragraph 2 to back up this view?

**5** The writer refers to her son, Peter, in paragraph 1. Find two other places in the article where she refers to **her own experience** to back up her view.

**6** The writer describes Peter and his class mates poring over the Argos catalogue (paragraph 4). What **extra detail** does she give to show the power of the Argos advertising?

## Reading for meaning

**7** The article begins with two questions. What **effect** do these have on the reader? **Give reasons** for your view.

**8** The newspaper article is mostly written in **formal** language. However, there are examples of **informal** language, such as contracted words and a conversational style.

**a)** Find an example of **conversational language** in paragraph 2.

**b)** Find an example of **contracted words** in paragraph 3.

**9** Why is the final paragraph an **effective end** to the article?

### Grammar for reading

**Conversational language** is the language of speech rather than writing. It is more informal and includes **contracted words**. For example: 'Go and fetch 'im' instead of 'Go and fetch him' or 'He doesn't want to' instead of 'He does not want to'.

## Focus on: Organising paragraphs

The following questions ask you to look at the way the sentences in the newspaper article are organised into paragraphs.

Look back at question 1. There you found the main point of paragraph 2. So what does the other sentence in the paragraph do? It backs up the main point by giving a reason:

**Main point:** adverts are now targeting seven-year-olds

New research by Harris Interactive shows that seven-year-olds are old enough to be a target consumer for youth market advertising. The idea is, apparently, get 'em young and then when they're old enough to spend, they will be indoctrinated in the delights of, well, probably Sunny Delight.

**Other sentence:** the reason for targeting seven-year-olds is to train them to spend later

S10 **10** Look at paragraph 4. Then, **write a simple sentence** explaining how the **main point** is backed up by the rest of the paragraph. Start like this:

'The main point made is that the writer's son and his friends love looking at the Argos catalogue. We know this because we are told they...'

**11** **a)** In pairs, find the **main point** of paragraph 3.

**b)** Then work out how the rest of the paragraph **supports** that point.

Remember: other sentences in a paragraph can back up the main point in three different ways (see page 148).

### Grammar for reading

A **paragraph** is a group of sentences that are all about the same topic. In an argument text, each new point has a separate paragraph. This helps the reader to follow the argument.

## Key Writing

**12** Write a **two-paragraph argument** on why toy advertising on TV should not be banned.

**a)** Choose **two points** from the following:

- Toy advertising is fun and does no harm.
- Children need to know about new toys on the market.
- Children are consumers just as adults are.
- Children take into account the power of advertising.

**b)** Decide how you will organise your first paragraph. What will the **opening sentence** of your argument be? Will you use a question to catch the reader's attention? Or will you lead off with your first main point?

**c)** Give a **reason** or use an **example** from your own experience to back up your main point.

**d)** Repeat b) and c) for your second paragraph.

# Pen pal dangers

## Aims

- Read a magazine article advising you about pen pals
- Explore how advice texts are written
- Analyse two important features of informal language
- Write a piece of advice in a style that suits the audience (Wr17)

**The following text comes from a teen magazine.**

## Pen Pal Dangers

*Thought putting pen to paper was a harmless way of making a new mate? Maybe not – as mizz discovers…*

Having a pen pal is a fantastic way to make new mates from different places. By meeting through official school schemes or exchanges where teachers can make sure everything is above board, pen pals can become friends for life. But the fact is, meeting someone via an internet club or through a magazine does have risks.

Take meeting someone creepy online. It's awful, but you can log off quick sharp. If you've written letters to them, however, that person's got your address, as well as loads of info about you that you've let them in on. It'd be like texting summat really personal to your best mate, then realising someone else had read it instead. So make sure that you get sussed before you start scribbling…

## Pen pal pointers

First off, don't panic and ring up your pen pal to accuse them of being an impostor. Nearly all people who write'll be
25 genuine, but it's important to follow *mizz*'s safety tips:

- You might get over 100 replies, but don't try to juggle too many. Go through 'em with your folks and pick a couple you'd like to be friends with.
- Take your pen pal friendship slowly. There's no need to
30 tell them every little fact about yourself until you know them properly.
- Don't ever give out your address or phone number without checking with your parents first. The best thing to do is get your folks to call the parents of your future
35 pen pal to check everything's cool.
- Make sure that you tell your parents immediately if you read something that makes you feel uncomfortable. You can then tackle the problem together.

And remember – as a *mizz* pen pal, we don't give your
40 address out to any old bod with a fancy stationery set. No personal details appear in the mag. We send you details of your wannabe pen pals and you pick who you want to write to.

**via** through

**impostor** someone pretending to be someone else

# Key Reading

## Advice texts

This is an **advice** text. Its **purpose** is to advise the reader to do (or not to do) something.

The main features of an advice text are:

- It includes a **series of points** in a **logical order**, for example, 'First off, don't panic and ring up your pen pal to accuse them of being an impostor.'
- The **design** helps to make the structure of the advice clear, for example, the safety tips are written as bullet points.
- It uses **direct address**, with commands to the reader or the words 'you' or 'your', for example, 'It's awful, but you can log off quick sharp.'

### Grammar for reading

**Direct address** is the term used when the writer speaks directly to the reader, for example, 'Tell your parents immediately', 'Don't panic'.

1 **What point** is the writer making in paragraph 1 (lines 3–8)? Why is the start of the article a good place to make this point?

2 Using **subheadings** helps the reader find their way around the text. Find the subheading 'Pen pal pointers'. What job does it do?

**3** How many times are the words 'you' and 'your' used in paragraph 2 (lines 9–21)? What is the **effect** of this?

## Purpose

**4** The purpose of an advice text is to advise the reader to act in a particular way. What do you think is the **main purpose** of this magazine article?

- to tell readers how to get a pen pal
- to give them safety tips when chatting online
- to give them safety tips when finding a pen pal
- to advise them not to get a pen pal through a magazine.

Point to the evidence in the text that supports your answer.

The magazine article is made up of two different sections. Each has a slightly different purpose, but both are important parts of the advice:

Bullet point list of **safety tips** to follow when getting a pen pal

Some **background information**:

- why having a pen pal is great
- how it can be dangerous

**5** In **which order** has the writer put these two different sections? Can you explain why?

## Reading for meaning

The advice starts with this sentence: 'Having a pen pal is a fantastic way to make new mates from different places.' The underlined words are **adjectives**. They help give a sentence a particular tone or mood.

**6** What **mood** is the writer trying to create with these adjectives? Positive and upbeat? Thoughtful? Sad?

**7** The third sentence **breaks this mood** (lines 6–8). What point is the writer making now? What is the mood now?

The word 'But' at the start of the second sentence is a **connective**. It is doing an important job:

positive statement about having pen pals

The connective 'but' signals to the reader that a different view is coming up in this sentence

...pen pals can become friends for life. But the fact is, meeting someone via an internet club or through a magazine does have risks.

statement advising you that there may be risks involved

**8** Connectives are also useful in the middle of sentences. Discuss with a partner **what job 'but' is doing** in paragraph 2: 'Take meeting someone creepy online. It's awful, *but* you can log off quick sharp.'

### Grammar for reading

**Adjectives** are describing words. They give more information about the nouns that they go with, for example, 'a *red* book', 'the *fierce* animal'.

**Connectives** are words that show how one sentence or clause is connected to another, for example, 'and', 'therefore', 'but'.

## Focus on: Informal language

Writers must always remember who their audience is. The audience of *mizz* magazine is young teenage girls. So the writer uses **informal language** to 'speak to' this audience.

One common feature of informal language is the use of **contracted words**. You can usually spot a contracted word by the apostrophe. This tells you that one or more letters have been missed out. For example:

- you're = you [a]re
- I'd = I [woul]d.

## Watch out!

Sometimes an apostrophe may show **possession** instead, for example, Mike's book.

Another common feature of informal language is the use of **conversational language**. This is language that is normally spoken rather than written, for example, 'mates', 'quick sharp', 'sussed'.

**9** Read through the four bullet points carefully with a partner. List the informal language that you find. Put it in a chart with two columns, like this:

Were there any words or phrases that you wanted to put in both columns?

| Contractions | Conversational language |
|---|---|
| don't | first off |
| write'll | |

## Further help

Childnet International ensures that the Internet is a safe place for young people. Their website is www.chatdanger.com.

Children who need to speak to someone in private can telephone ChildLine (0800 1111).

# Key Writing

**10** Read the 'Further help' box. The editor at *mizz* needs you to rewrite it so that it matches the friendly style of the rest of the article.

**a)** Decide how to order the advice in the box.

**b)** Then rewrite 'Further help'.

Remember:

- Use contractions and conversational language.
- Address the reader directly – use 'you' and commands.
- Present the heading in an eye-catching way.

# ④ Unit 7 Assignment: Celebrity of the year

## Assessment Focuses

- AF4 Construct paragraphs and use cohesion within and between paragraphs
- AF7 Select appropriate and effective vocabulary

**You:** are taking part in a class debate.

**Your task:** to write a short speech proposing your favourite celebrity as 'Celebrity of the Year'.

## Stage 1

Choose your celebrity. He or she could be a pop star, a sportsperson, or an actor – anyone in the media, in fact.

Now think about why you admire them. Make a list of three qualities that make them your top celebrity. For example:

Celebrity: Kylie Minogue
My celebrity of the year because of:

- her songs
- her looks
- her success

## Stage 2

You are going to write one paragraph on each quality. First of all, decide which order you want the paragraphs to go in. Remember that you should have a powerful ending. You may want to save your best quality until last.

## Stage 3

Now draft your three paragraphs.

Remember to:

- Make your **main point** early in each paragraph.
- Use the other sentences in each paragraph to back up the main point. They can do this by giving a **reason**, by giving **evidence**, or by giving an **example** or **more detail**.

For example:

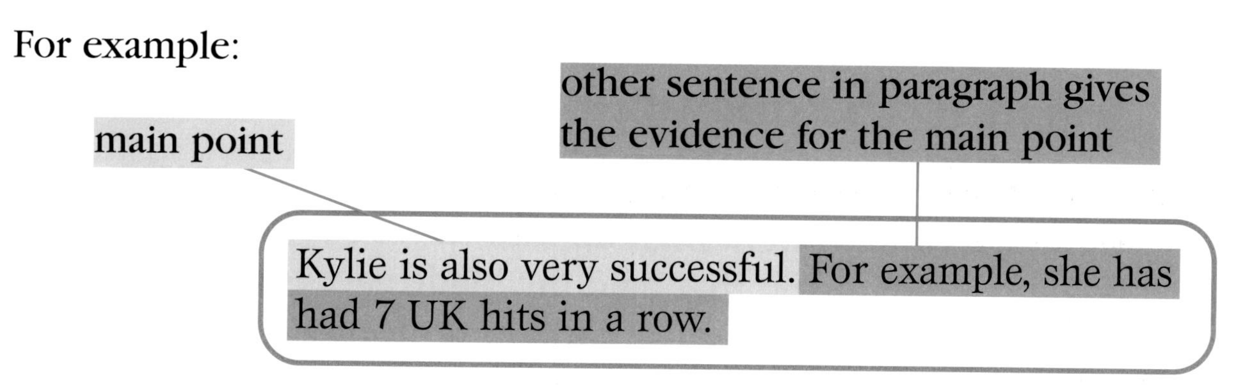


Now read through your speech again and check how effective it is. Remember that this speech will be read aloud. It must sound effective. Can you make any words more powerful or interesting?

For example:

change 'very' to 'incredibly'

Kylie is also incredibly successful. Has anyone else had 7 smash hits in the UK all in a row?

change 'hits' to 'smash hits'

use of question to grab audience

# Unit 8 Past lives

## 1 A visit to the doctor

### Aims

- Read from an autobiography
- Learn how to skim and scan (R1, R2)
- Learn how to extend sentences (Wr8)

---

**In *Boy*, Roald Dahl (1916–1990) recounts important events that happened to him. A visit to the doctor was one of them.**

### A visit to the doctor

The tiny blade flashed in the bright light and disappeared into my mouth. It went high up into the roof of my mouth, and the hand that held the blade gave four or five very quick little twists and the next moment, out of my mouth into the basin came tumbling a whole mass of flesh and blood.

I was too shocked and outraged to do anything but yelp. I was horrified by the huge red lumps that had fallen out of my mouth into the white basin and my first thought was that the doctor had cut out the whole of the middle of my head.

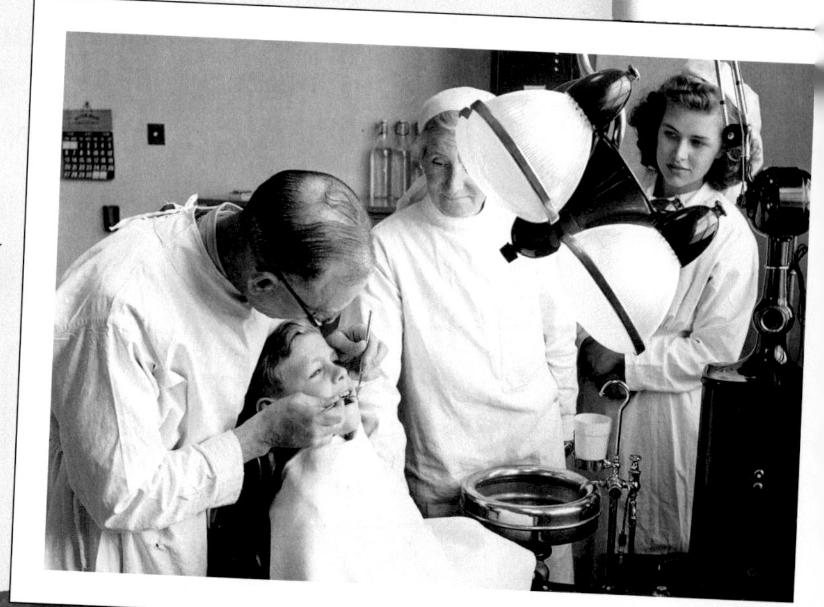

'Those were your adenoids,' I heard the doctor saying.
I sat there gasping. The roof of my mouth seemed to be
20 on fire. I grabbed my mother's arm and held on to it
tight. I couldn't believe that anyone would do this to me.
'Stay where you are,' the doctor said. 'You'll be all right
in a minute.'
Blood was still coming out of my mouth and dripping
25 into the basin the nurse was holding. 'Spit it all out,' she
said, 'there's a good boy.'
'You'll be able to breathe much better through your
nose after this,' the doctor said.
The nurse wiped my lips and washed my face with a
30 wet flannel. Then they lifted me out of the chair and
stood me on my feet. I felt a bit groggy.
'We'll get you home,' my mother said, taking my hand.
Down the stairs we went and on to the street. We
started walking. I said *walking*. No trolley-car or taxi. We
35 walked the full half-hour journey back to my
grandparents' house, and when we arrived at last, I can
remember as clearly as anything my grandmother saying,
'Let him sit down in the chair and rest for a while. After
all, he's had an operation.'
40 Someone placed a chair for me beside my
grandmother's armchair, and I sat down. My
grandmother reached over and covered one of my hands
in both of hers. 'That won't be the last time you'll go to a
doctor in your life,' she said. 'And with a bit of luck, they
45 won't do you too much harm.'
That was in 1924, and taking out a child's adenoids,
and often the tonsils as well, without any anaesthetic was
common practice in those days. I wonder, though, what
you would think if some doctor did that to you today.

**adenoids** large mass of tissue between the back of the nose and the throat

**tonsils** two small masses of tissue in the throat near the back of the tongue

**trolley-car** public transport: a tram, run on electricity from an overhead cable

# Key Reading

## Autobiography

This text is an **autobiography**. It is a **recount**, in which the writer tells his life story. Its **purpose** is to recount or tell the reader about a series of events – in this case, Roald Dahl's early memories. The main features of an autobiography are:

- It is mainly told in the **past tense**, for example, 'The tiny blade *flashed*...'
- It uses **time connectives** (words that tell the order of events), for example, '*Then* they lifted me out of the chair...', '*That was in 1924*...'
- It is written in the **first person** (singular 'I' and plural 'we'), for example, '*I* was too shocked...'
- It includes **facts**, for example, 'Those were your adenoids...'
- It includes **opinions**, for example, 'I couldn't believe that anyone would do this to me.'

**1** a) Find an example of the **first person singular** 'I' in paragraph 2.

b) **Who** does 'I' refer to?

**2** a) Sometimes the first person plural 'we' is used. **Find an example** on page 163.

b) **Who** does 'we' refer to?

**3** a) Read the following sentence and say which word is the **verb**: 'I grabbed my mother's arm...'

b) Is the verb in the **present** or **past tense**? How can you tell?

**4** A **time connective** is used in line 24 to show how one event leads to another. What is this time connective?

## Purpose

**5** Why do you think that Roald Dahl wrote about this event? There could be more than one reason. Discuss which of these you think are likely:

- It was a memory he was unable to forget.
- He wanted to warn people about doctors.
- He thought his readers would be interested in it.
- He wanted to shock his readers.

## Reading for meaning

### Skimming the text

When you read a text quickly the first time, you can get a rough idea of **what it is about** and **how it is told**. This means you **skim** the text.

R1

**6** What can you remember from your first reading of the extract from *Boy*? Is the text **mainly** about:

- the kindness of the writer's grandmother
- Dahl's adenoids being taken out
- the doctor's skill?

Questions 7 and 8 are about the order in which things happened. Try to remember.

**7** Are we told about the walk home **early on** or **later** in the text?

**8** **In what order** do the following events occur in the text:

- his grandmother held his hand
- the operation
- the nurse washed his face?

### Scanning the text

If you want to find a piece of information in a text, you can **scan** it. This means skipping words to find what you are looking for. **Scanning** is a good way to get information quickly. For example, to find out what kind of operation Roald Dahl had, you could scan through the paragraphs until you find a key word such as 'adenoids'. For example, '"Those were your *adenoids*," I heard the doctor saying.'

R2

**9** **Scan the text** for the following:

- the year that Roald Dahl had the operation
- what kind of transport the writer *could* have used to get home
- why the operation was performed.

## Focus on: Keeping up the tension

When writing you may want to keep some information back until the end of a sentence or paragraph. You can do this by varying the way you start your sentences. For example, Roald Dahl does this in paragraph 1 when he writes:

> … out of my mouth into the basin came tumbling *a whole mass of flesh and blood.*

Dahl could have written:

> …*a whole mass of flesh and blood* came tumbling out of my mouth into the basin.

By leaving the part that has the greatest impact until the end, the tension is kept up in the reader's mind.

S1c **10** **Change this sentence around** so that the tension is kept up: 'Maggots crawled from a purple gash when he slowly turned the body over.'

### Adding description

When writing you can also extend sentences by adding description at the end. For example:

> He stared at the deep wound.

By adding to this sentence, a more interesting description is created:

> He stared at the deep wound, *spurting with blood.*

## Key Writing

**11** **a)** Read the recount below about an accident. **Add detail** to the sentences that need finishing.

**b)** Try changing some of the sentences around so they **begin with the detail** you have added.

**c)** Add some **time connectives** to the events so that the order in which they happened is clear, for example, 'then', 'when', 'all at once', 'next', 'a few moments later', 'at last'.

The huge dog ran down the hall, *barking…*

Molly was directly in his path.

She was flung into the air, *landing…*

Her arm was twisted behind her back, *hanging…*

She lay still for a moment, her eyes shut.

Slowly she opened them and began *screaming…*

# 2 It was long ago

## Aims

- Read a poem
- Learn about rhyme and rhythm
- Find repetition in the poem (R14)
- Write rhyming couplets (Wr8)

---

***It Was Long Ago* is a poem by Eleanor Farjeon (1881–1965) that has stood the test of time. As you read it, try to think why it is still read today.**

It Was Long Ago

I'll tell you, shall I, something I remember?
Something that still means a great deal to me.
It was long ago.

A dusty road in summer I remember,
5 A mountain, and an old house, and a tree
That stood, you know,

Behind the house. An old woman I remember
In a red shawl with a grey cat on her knee
Humming under a tree.

10 She seemed the oldest thing I can remember,
But then perhaps I was not more than three.
It was long ago.

I dragged on the dusty road, and I remember
How the old woman looked over the fence at me
15 And seemed to know

How it felt to be three, and called out, I remember
'Do you like bilberries and cream for tea?'
I went under the tree

And while she hummed, and the cat purred, I remember
20 How she filled a saucer with berries and cream for me
So long ago,

Such berries and such cream as I remember
I never had seen before, and never see
To-day, you know.

25 And that is almost all I can remember,
The house, the mountain, the grey cat on her knee,
Her red shawl, and the tree,

And the taste of the berries, the feel of the sun I remember,
30 And the smell of everything that used to be
So long ago,

Till the heat on the road outside again I remember,
And how the long dusty road seemed to have for me
No end, you know.

35 This is the farthest thing I can remember.
It won't mean much to you. It does to me.
Then I grew up, you see.

## Key Reading

### Poems

This text is a **poem**. Its **purpose** is to explore feelings and ideas.

A poem is made up of **images**, **rhythm** and **form**.

- The **images** are the pictures made by the words.
- The **rhythm** is like the beat in music.
- The **form** is the framework or pattern of the poem. Poems are written in lines not sentences.

Other important features of poems are:

- Some poems **rhyme** (for example, doom/gloom/tomb).
- Some poems are **free verse**. They have lines of different lengths with different rhythms. (Some free verse contains rhyme.)

**1** Read the first verse of *It Was Long Ago* again. Is the poem written:

- in the first person 'I'
- in the second person 'you'
- in the third person 'he' or 'she'?

**2** **a)** Do you think the person **telling** the story is:

- a young child
- an older child
- a teenager
- an adult?

**b)** How can you tell?

## Purpose

The poem *It Was Long Ago* explores feelings and ideas about childhood.

**3** Does the last line of the poem make you feel:

- sad
- thoughtful
- like smiling
- a mixture of feelings?

**4** **Write a sentence** to explain your feelings. Use this sentence frame:
'The last line of the poem made me feel…because…'

## Reading for meaning

The poem is told like a story. By repeating the words 'I remember' throughout the poem, the poet reminds the reader about the importance of her memories.

The same **rhyme pattern** is also used throughout. For example, rhyme comes on the middle line of each verse.

I'll tell you, shall I, something I remember?
Something that still means a great deal to me.
It was long ago.

A dusty road in summer I remember
A mountain, and an old house, and a tree
That stood, you know,

**5** Work out the rhyme pattern in the verses on the following page. Remember, a rhyme has to sound the same, but does not have to be spelled the same. The rhyme pattern has been started for you.

| | |
|---|---|
| I'll tell you, shall I, something I remember? | **a** |
| Something that still means a great deal to me. | **b** |
| It was long ago. | |
| | |
| A dusty road in summer I remember | **a** |
| A mountain, and an old house, and a tree | |
| That stood, you know, | |

**6** **a)** Find **another word or phrase** that is repeated in these verses.

**b)** What **effect** does this have?

R14 Focus on: Rhythm

All speech has **rhythm**. You can work this out by counting the syllables (or parts) in certain words and by listening to find out which syllables are stressed.

For example, the word 'remember' has three syllables: re-mem-ber. When you say 'remember', the stress is put on the middle syllable. The other two syllables in 'remember' are unstressed. In this way, the rhythms of speech are made up of **stressed** and **unstressed** syllables.

**7** **a)** Write down these words from the poem and **split them into syllables**: *something, ago, dusty, perhaps, bilberries*

**b)** Which syllable is **stressed** in each word?

In some poems you can feel the rhythm easily.

**8** **a)** This is the first line from verse 4. Read it and **gently tap out the beat**.

'She seemed the oldest thing I can remember,'

**b)** Now read the second line *without* tapping out the beat. Does it have the **same rhythm**?

**c)** Find the **third line** in the verse. Does it have the same rhythm?

**9** **a)** Choose another verse from the poem. Read it naturally. Does it have the same **pattern of rhythm** as the fourth verse?

**b)** Which of these describes the **rhythm** in the poem?

- No verse is the same as another.
- Some verses are the same.
- There is rhythm in some verses.
- The rhythm of each verse is repeated.

# Key Writing

### Grammar for reading

A **rhyming couplet** is two lines of poetry that have the same rhyme at the end. For example:

> In front of us, the great school *gate*,
> And all the thrill of being *late*.

**11** a) **Think of a memory** from your early childhood. It might be linked to:

- holidays
- starting school
- moving home
- a sporting event

Wr8

b) Plan and **write a short poem** of three rhyming couplets to sum up your memory. Your couplets can be short or long but give the lines the same rhythm.

Choose from the following rhymes if you need to:

- school/rule
- goal/roll/stole
- day/stay/say/away
- gone/song/strong
- rain/again/train
- learn/return

For example,

> That breaktime I was on a roll
> I'd just scored our team's first goal.

# 3 King Arthur: the truth (probably)

Aims

- Read an analysis text
- Learn how points are presented and questions asked
- Learn about connectives of cause, effect and contrast (W20)
- Take part in a group discussion about evidence (S&L1)

---

**The following case study of King Arthur is taken from a children's book that analyses stories from history against real source material.**

## King Arthur's Story

### What's the story?

You mean you don't know? Well, there's this young lad. Called 'Wart' by his brother on account of being small and spotty, probably. One day a long time ago he sees a bloomin' great big rock. Thing is, it's got this 5 magical-looking sword sticking out of it, and if you pull it out you get to be Big Chief (well, King) of the Britons. But nobody, not even the biggest muscle-men, can remove it. But 'Wart' wanders up, and pulls it out, like it's a wobbly tooth. And so the legend is born. Arthur (ex-Wart), King of the Britons, leader of the Knights of the Round Table, has arrived.

### 10 Sounds a bit unlikely

Are you questioning the great Walt Disney? This is a scene from the animated film, *'The Sword in the Stone'*. It's a bit like all those other films about Arthur. You know the ones – *'Excalibur'* and, err, *'Monty Python and the Holy Grail'*. Plus, *'King Arthur'*. You must have heard of that one!

15 Well, usually Arthur and his knights sit around a Round Table (to show how equal they all are). Plus, there's Arthur's wife, the beautiful Guinivere – who has an 'affair' with Launcelot (one of Arthur's knights). And they all live happily at the castle of Camelot (well, Arthur wasn't that pleased, obviously).

## Great for films, but is any of it true? Did Arthur even exist?

Let's look at the evidence:

Source 1: **De Excidio Britanniae (6th century history book)**
Who: Gildas' (some British guy who wrote in Latin)
What: He mentions an important soldier, who might have been Arthur, at this great big battle in 5th century Roman Britain.
BUT...there's no mention of him being a 'king'
AND...not definitely mentioned by name.

Source 2: **The Modena Cathedral Carving, Italy (around 1120)**
Who: Search me
What: Carving of a violent-looking bloke on horseback carrying a pointy thing (it's a lance, you idiot!). Funny writing reads *Artus de Bretania* (it's Latin, you fool!). This means 'Arthur of Britannia' (alright, clever clogs).
BUT...*everyone* knew about Arthur – he was the Beckham of his day (except he didn't play football, and had been dead – if he existed – six hundred years, so the carver may just have liked the story).

## Is that it?

Are you joking? Everyone has something to say about Arthur!

Source 3: **'Historia Regum Britanniae' (another old history book– why can't these people write in English?)**
Who: Geoffrey of Monmouth (12th century)
What: He includes a romantic hero called Arthur.
BUT...much of this 'history' was probably made-up.

Source 4: **Arthur's grave at Glastonbury**
Who: Silly question
What: In 1191, in an old oak coffin, monks found the bodies of a huge man and a woman with golden hair. A cross made of lead inside read: 'Here lies the illustrious King Arthur buried in the Isle of Avalon.'
BUT...It's probably a forgery! Historians reckon the monks did it 'cos they needed money. And it worked. As a result, it brought the abbey immense fame and wealth.

## So, what are you saying?

We can reveal exclusively that we really don't know. Ok, there *may* have been an important soldier with a name like 'Arthur'. And he *might* have been around pointing sharp things at folk in the 5th or 6th centuries. But, most of the evidence is in the form of stories, poems or art. There are no bones or contemporary drawings of Arthur, as far as we know.

## Key Reading

### Analysis texts

This text is an **analysis**. Its **purpose** is to **study information or ideas closely**, in this case to see if the information is **reliable**.

The main features of an analysis text are:

- It is told mainly in the **present tense**, although it sometimes switches to the **past tense** to give background information. For example:
  - when discussing the evidence the writer says, '*It's* probably a forgery' (present tense)
  - when saying how and when the evidence was discovered, the writer says, '...monks *found* the bodies of a huge man and a woman…' (past tense).
- Points are made clearly and backed up with **evidence**. For example, the evidence in the extract comes from historical sources such as facts, pictures and diagrams (like the Modena Cathedral Carving).
- It uses connectives to do with **cause and effect**, for example, '…*As a result*, it brought the abbey immense fame and wealth' (the effect).

**1** Who is the **subject** of this analysis?

**2** **a)** How many **sources** of evidence are discussed?

**b)** How **old** are each of the sources?

*A humorous version of King Arthur's story in* Monty Python and the Holy Grail

**3** Find an example of a **present tense verb** in the first heading.

**4** The writer also uses the past tense. Find an example of a **past tense verb** in this sentence from the text: 'BUT…much of this "history" was probably made-up.'

## Purpose

**5** This analysis is about an historical figure, but **what is it trying to prove**?

**6** Which of these **kinds of evidence** are looked at as sources?

- photos
- paintings
- books
- statues or carvings
- burial grounds
- letters

## Reading for meaning

**7** The analysis is laid out clearly. For example, it uses questions for some headings. Who do you think is supposed to be **asking** the questions?

R8

**8** The second question, 'Did Arthur even exist?' leads to the **main part of the analysis**.

**a)** What **evidence** is there in Source 1 that a person like Arthur lived in the 5th or 6th centuries?

**b)** Why is this evidence not very **reliable**?

**9** The evidence in Source 4 about Glastonbury seems very powerful. Why is it **not as reliable as it seems**?

**10** The writer uses a funny, jokey style in places. Find at least two examples of **jokes or comic language** under Source 2.

*Launcelot with Arthur and Guinevere in* King Arthur

## Focus on: Using connectives of cause, effect and contrast

You can use connectives to link **cause** (reason) and **effect** (what happens). For example:

cause

connective

> We wanted to find out if Arthur was a real person, so we studied the carving.

effect

You could also write the sentence this way:

> We studied the carving **because** we wanted to find out if Arthur was a real person.

**11** What word has **changed** in the sentence?

**12** Choose the right **connective** (either 'so' or 'because') to turn these two sentences into one sentence. Write the sentence down and remember to drop the full stop and capital letter.

> The monks wanted to make Glastonbury famous. They discovered Arthur's grave.

The other main type of connective used in the extract is one that shows two contrasting points of view. Usually, this appears as 'BUT…' in the text. The connective 'however' could also be used to contrast two points of view.

Here is another source of evidence and a sentence suggesting that this evidence is **unreliable**:

> Thomas Malory wrote a whole book about Arthur in 1470. It wasn't based on historical facts.

**13** Write these two sentences as **one sentence**, using the connective 'but' or 'however'.

## Key Speaking and Listening

**14** In groups, discuss the **evidence** about King Arthur.

**a)** Decide whether there really was a King Arthur. In your discussion, use connectives such as 'but', 'however', 'so' and 'because'.

**b)** Discuss **why** the legend of Arthur has survived.

**c)** After the discussion, consider how well you:

- **explained** your views
- **listened** to the views of others in the group
- used helpful **connectives**
- referred to clues or **evidence** from the sources.

# 4 Unit 8 Assignment: The historian's analysis

## Assessment Focuses

- AF3 Organise and present whole texts effectively, sequencing and structuring information, ideas and events

**You:** are an historian. You study evidence about the past.

**Your task:** to write an analysis and an assessment of the evidence. When you assess the evidence you must decide how useful it is to an historian.

## Stage 1

You have a list of questions to refer to.

**Information**

a) What kind of evidence is it? (For example, an object, a picture or written evidence?)

b) Where does it come from? (For example, a book or a newspaper?)

c) When was it made or written?

d) Who wrote it?

e) Who or what was it about?

f) Are there any interviews? If so, who with?

**Quality of the evidence**

g) What weaknesses does it have?

h) What useful things does it tell us about the past?

i) Is it good evidence? Why?

## Source A

...they are commonly known by the name of 'mud-larks' (and) sometimes wade up to their middle through the mud left on the (river) shore...The mud-larks collect whatever they happen to find, such as coals, bits of old iron, rope, bones, and copper nails...The coals...they sell to the poor people of the neighbourhood.

From *London Labour and the London Poor*
by Henry Mayhew, 1861.

## Source B

'It is very cold in winter' he said, 'to stand in the mud without shoes'...He had been three years mud-larking, and supposed he should remain a mud-lark all his life. What else could he be?'

Comments from a boy aged nine in *London Labour and the London Poor* by Henry Mayhew, 1861.

## Stage 2

Check the evidence against the questions and write your notes. For example:

Information about Source B
a) Written evidence
b) A book
c) 1861

## Stage 3

Use your notes to write two paragraphs under the following **sub-headings**:

- Information I found out
- Quality of the evidence.

In your writing you should:

- turn your notes into **full sentences**
- write mainly in the **present tense**
- write in the **past tense** only when referring to the past (for example, 'It was written in…')
- use the **connectives** 'so' and 'because'.

You may like to start with this writing frame:
Paragraph 1: 'Source A is written evidence that comes from…'
Paragraph 2: 'Overall I think that…'

### Challenge

Redraft your account to improve the style.

- Lengthen your sentences by using more connectives. For example, 'Source A is written evidence that comes from…*by*…*in*…'
- Use a verb to begin a sentence. For example, instead of writing: 'An interview is included…', write 'Included is an interview…'

# Unit 9 Sporting challenge

## 1 Ellen MacArthur's inspiration

### Aims

- Read a profile about a famous yachtswoman
- Learn how to search for key information (R1)
- Learn how to make clear notes from information you have read (R4)

**This first text is from an article about the young yachtswoman, Ellen MacArthur, from a BBC webpage. It describes how she became a sailor.**

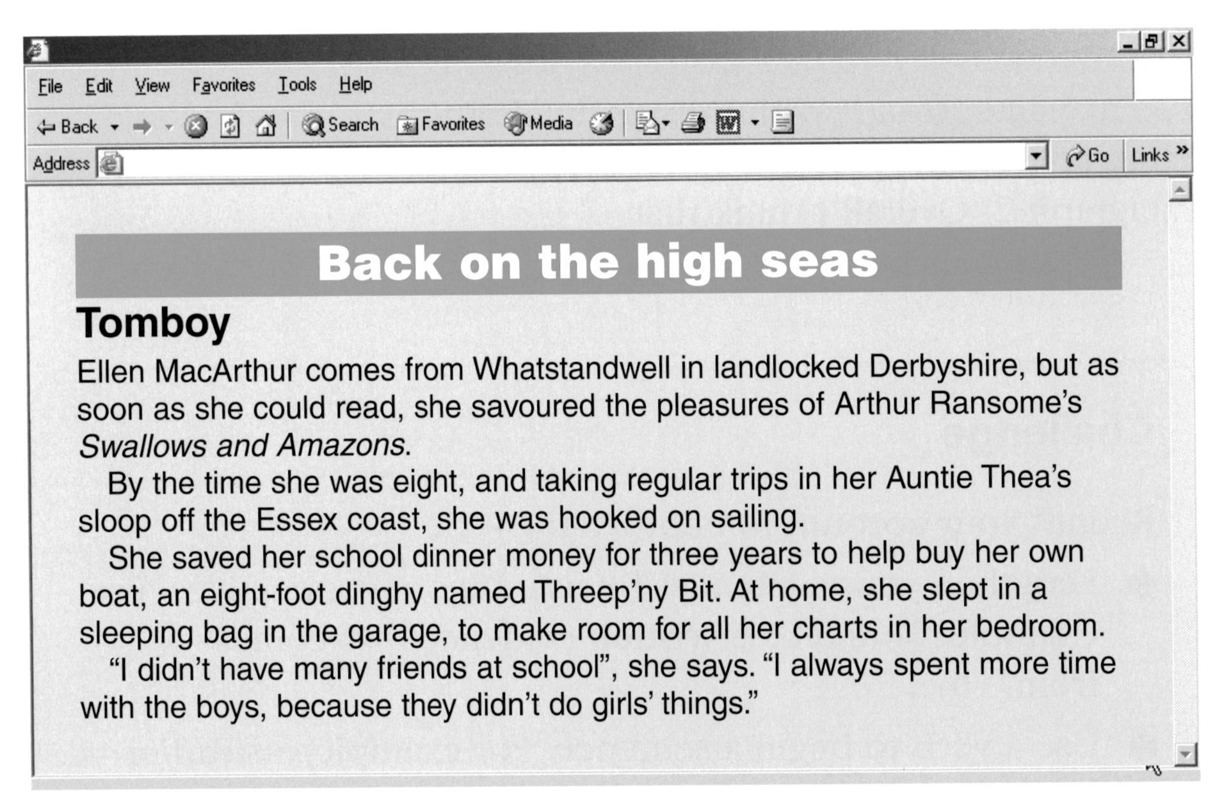


## Back on the high seas

### Tomboy

Ellen MacArthur comes from Whatstandwell in landlocked Derbyshire, but as soon as she could read, she savoured the pleasures of Arthur Ransome's *Swallows and Amazons*.

By the time she was eight, and taking regular trips in her Auntie Thea's sloop off the Essex coast, she was hooked on sailing. (5)

She saved her school dinner money for three years to help buy her own boat, an eight-foot dinghy named Threep'ny Bit. At home, she slept in a sleeping bag in the garage, to make room for all her charts in her bedroom.

"I didn't have many friends at school", she says. "I always spent more time with the boys, because they didn't do girls' things." (10)

At 18, she sailed single-handed round Britain and won the Young Sailor of the Year award.

15 But it wasn't until she took part in a solo race across the Atlantic in 1997 that little Ellen, 5 ft 2 in with eyes of blue, attracted 20 major sponsorship, from Kingfisher, the stores group.

## Inspiration

It was Ellen's grandmother, Irene Lewis, who made it 25 possible to enter her first big race.

She left Ellen £5,000 in her will, enabling her to pay the entrance fee for the 30 *Vendee Globe*.

But her nan also provided inspiration. She was 82 when she graduated from Derby University despite 35 suffering from lung cancer. She died three months later.

This example of courage helped Ellen MacArthur to realise her dream and to tell her story in an autobiography, *Taking on the World*.

40 Now 26, she lives in a one-bedroom flat at Cowes on the Isle of Wight. But her emotional home is the sea.

**tomboy** a girl who behaves like a boy
**landlocked** land all around, not by the sea
***Swallows and Amazons*** a famous children's adventure book
**sloop** a type of sailing boat
**Threep'ny bit** short for 'three-penny bit' (old three pence coin)
**sponsorship** when a company pays to support someone
**inspiration** where the belief to do something comes from
**Vendee Globe** a round-the-world sailing race
**graduate** pass your degree at college or university

# Key Reading

## Recount texts

This text is a **recount.** Its **purpose** is to recount or **tell** the reader about a series of events.

The main **features** of a recount text are:

- It is mainly told in the past tense, for example, 'She sailed single-handed round Britain.'
- It describes events in **time order** (chronological order), for example, we are told that Ellen was sailing regularly 'by the time she was eight'.
- It uses **time connectives** (words that tell us the order of events), for example, 'by the time', 'until', etc.

S13b

1 a) **Who** is being described in this extract?

b) What **sport or activity** is she famous for?

2 Find **two past tense verbs** in the third paragraph.

3 Find any other mention of her **age**. Does this come before or after the mention of her being 8 and 18?

4 Find at least **one time connective** in the paragraph beginning, 'But her nan…' (page 187).

## Purpose

**5** What do you think the **main purpose** of this text is?
**Discuss** these possibilities:

- to show that girls are as tough as boys
- to tell us about Ellen MacArthur's struggles and how she was inspired to succeed
- to make us aware that older people can be inspiring.

## Reading for meaning

**6** **Who** is this text mostly about?:

**a)** Ellen

**b)** Ellen's gran

**7** **Sub-headings** are a key feature of this text.
Remember, a sub-heading goes underneath a main title or heading. It is usually smaller in size than the main title.

> **My Favourite Pet**
>
> **Name and looks**
>
> My dog is called Homer. He is a golden Labrador.
>
> **Feeding**
>
> Homer likes to eat meat chunks and gnaw on old bones.

The text is divided into two sections, each with a **sub-heading**

One of the article's sub-headings is 'Tomboy'.

**a)** **Who** does it refer to?

**b)** How do you know?

**8** The text starts with Ellen's early life. **Where** does she live now?

**9** Ellen has just written a book about her life. What is it **called**?

## Focus on: Finding information and making clear notes

Imagine that you have to write an article about a sports person you find inspiring (someone who has faced problems and overcome them, like Ellen MacArthur). To do this, you need to find the **right information**.

R1 **10** Which of these pieces of information would be useful to your article?

| Ellen's nan was 82 when she graduated from Derby University. | OR | Ellen saved her school dinner money for three years to help buy her own boat. |
|---|---|---|

R4 **11** One way of making notes is to make a list. This means you:

- **cut out** any words or phrases that **you don't need**
- **shorten** or make information **more simple**.

Like this:

~~By the time she was~~ eight, ~~and taking regular trips in her~~ Auntie ~~Thea's~~ sloop ~~off the~~ Essex coast, ~~she was hooked on sailing~~.

Becomes:

*Ellen, 8, in Aunt's boat, Essex coast*

Here's one more thing Ellen did that was inspiring. Turn it into a **simple note**:

*At 18, she sailed single-handed round Britain and won the Young Sailor of the Year award.*

## Key writing

**12** Now **complete the list** of things Ellen did that were inspiring.

Remember, these are **notes**, so:

- use only the **key words** you need
- **shorten and simplify** longer phrases or words (for example 'Aunt's boat' not 'Auntie Thea's sloop').

# 2 Bend it like Beckham

## Aims

- Read an extract from a novel
- Develop the skill of looking for key words
- Learn more about speech punctuation (S7)
- Write your own text using direct speech

---

**The following text is from a book by Narinder Dhami about Jess Bhamra, a British Indian girl who plays football. Her team is in a big final, but it is also her sister's wedding day. Jess's father has finally allowed Jess to play in the match. However, the game has already started…**

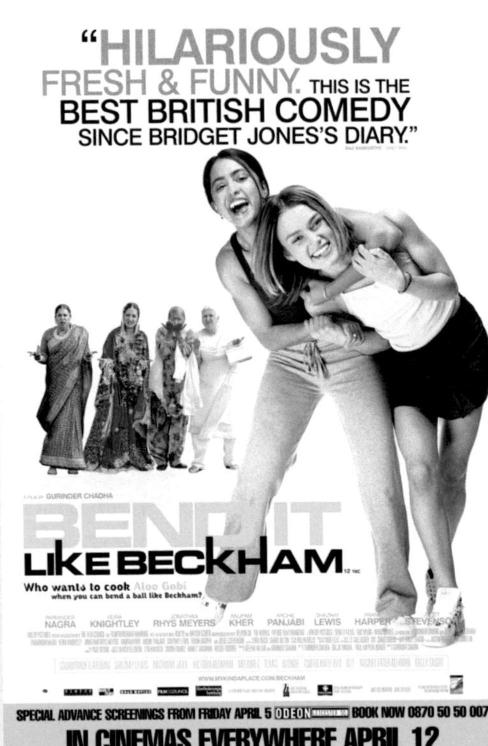


## Bend it like Beckham

My adrenaline was rocketing as I pushed my way through the crowd and vaulted over the barrier, rushing over to Joe who was standing shouting on the touchline. His face broke into a huge smile when he saw me, but he didn't stop to ask any questions.

'Start warming up, Bhamra,' he said, giving my shoulder a squeeze. 'We're one-nil down.'

One-nil down. That was a bit of a shock. Still, there was plenty of time for us to come back. We were only about twenty minutes into the first half.

I did my stretches, then jogged impatiently on the touchline, waiting for my chance to get on to the pitch. It came when Mel fouled one of the other team, and they got a free kick. I dashed on to the field as a sub, getting patted on the back and cheered by the other Harriers as I passed. Jules had only just noticed me, and her mouth dropped open in amazement.

'I'm so glad you came!' she yelled, giving me a huge hug. Relief surged through me. It was going to be OK.

Together, we lined up alongside the others to make a defensive wall, as one of the QPR players placed the ball for their free kick. They were only just outside the penalty area, and this was their chance to grab another goal. I could feel the blood rushing in my ears as I watched the player run up to take it. Being two down would be no joke. But the ball sailed over the top of the wall, and Charlie caught it safely.

Now that Jules and I were back in business as friends *and* team-mates, we played better than ever. Our passes were fast and sharp and accurate, and we moved smoothly down the pitch, almost reading each other's minds as the ball flew between us. We were ripping the heart out of the QPR defence. It was only a matter of time before we scored.

I watched as Mel passed the ball to Jules while we ran from the centre into the QPR half. I knew what Jules was going to do – and she did it. She let the ball roll through her legs to me, completely fooling the QPR defence. I picked it up quickly behind her, allowing Jules to run forward nearer to the goal, then I threaded a neat pass towards her. Jules was on to it in a flash, and a second later the ball was sitting in the corner of the net.

Jules screamed 'YES!' and ran round the pitch with her top over her head, showing off her sports bra. I couldn't stop laughing. Joe was going mad on the touchline, while the rest of us jumped on top of Jules, hugging her to death.

**adrenaline** a hormone that makes the heart beat faster and increases alertness

**sub** short for 'substitute', someone who takes the place of a player who has started the match

**Harriers** the name of Jess's football team

**QPR** Queens Park Rangers (a well-known London football team)

**defensive wall** a line of players who make a human wall to block a shot at goal

# Key Reading

## Narrative texts

This text is a **narrative.** Its **purpose** is to tell a **story.**

The main features of a narrative text are:

- It has a structure that includes an opening (**introduction**), a problem (**complication**), a dramatic moment when everything comes to a head (**crisis**) and an ending (**resolution**) when things are sorted out. For example, *Bend it like Beckham* has the following structure:

  **Introduction:** We find out about Jess and her love of football.
  **Complication:** Jess joins a football team secretly but her parents find out and are not happy.
  **Crisis:** Jess is set to play in a final but it is her sister's wedding.
  **Resolution:** Jess's dad finally allows her to play in the match.
- It has **characters** who the story is about. We often hear their words and thoughts in direct speech shown by speech marks. For example, 'Jules screamed "YES!"'. There is also a **narrator** who tells the story. In this case the narrator is the main character, Jess.
- It has **powerful description**. For example, 'We were *ripping the heart out* of the QPR defence.'

**1** The extract deals only with one very small part of the whole story.

**a)** Discuss **what happens** in this extract.

**b)** What is Jess's **problem** at the beginning of this extract?

**2** Find **one other example of direct speech** – someone talking to another person (look for speech marks).

**3** Powerful language in writing usually comes with the use of images – pictures created in the reader's mind. **What is the writer trying to tell us** when she says:

- 'We were ripping the heart out of the QPR defence.'
- 'I could feel the blood rushing in my ears as I watched the player run up.'

## Purpose

The **purpose** of *Bend it like Beckham* is to **tell a story** and to **entertain**. Two of the ways it does this are:

- By making the reader **want to know what will happen next**, both *during* the text and *after* it.
- By making the reader **interested in the characters and what they feel**.

## Reading for meaning

One way of finding information to answer a question about a text is to look at the **key words** in the question. This will help you to find the evidence in the text. For example:

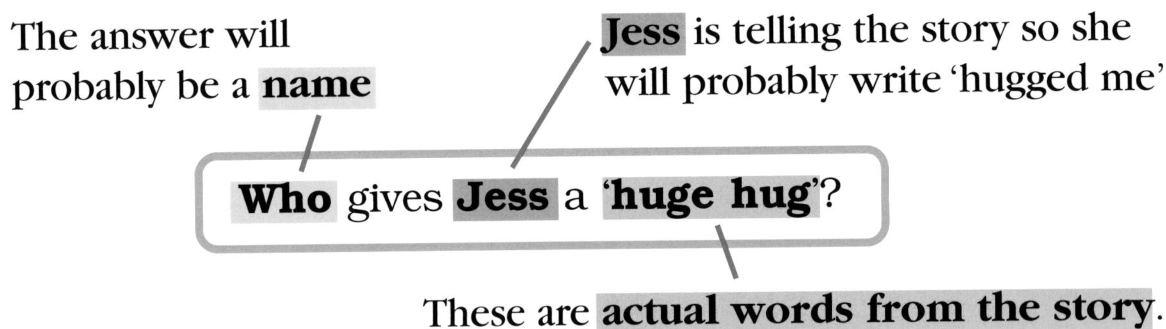


You can tell this because they are in inverted commas. So look for these words!

Sometimes the words in the question *are not* in the story but **similar** or **connected** words are. For example:

**What is the score** in the game when **Jess arrives**?

The answer will probably be a **number**

**'Jess arrives'** tells us that this is the start of the text, not the end. So look there for your answer

**4** **Answer these questions** on the extract in a group. Use the notes above to help you with the first two questions. Look for the key words in the last question and then answer it.

**a)** What is the score in the game when Jess arrives?

**b)** Who gives Jess a 'huge hug'?

**c)** Who catches the ball from the QPR free kick?

**5** Here are two possible sub-headings for two paragraphs:

- 'Defending the freekick'
- 'Making a goal for Jules'

Find the **most suitable paragraph** for each of these sub-headings.

**6** Which of these words would be best as a **sub-heading** for the last paragraphs?:

- 'Celebration'
- 'Despair'
- ' Anger'

## Focus on: How to punctuate speech in longer sentences

Speech is **punctuated** in the following ways:

- by using **speech marks**
- by stating **who is speaking**
- by putting any punctuation to do with the speech **in front of the final speech marks**
- by **starting** each **new speaker's** lines as **a new paragraph**.

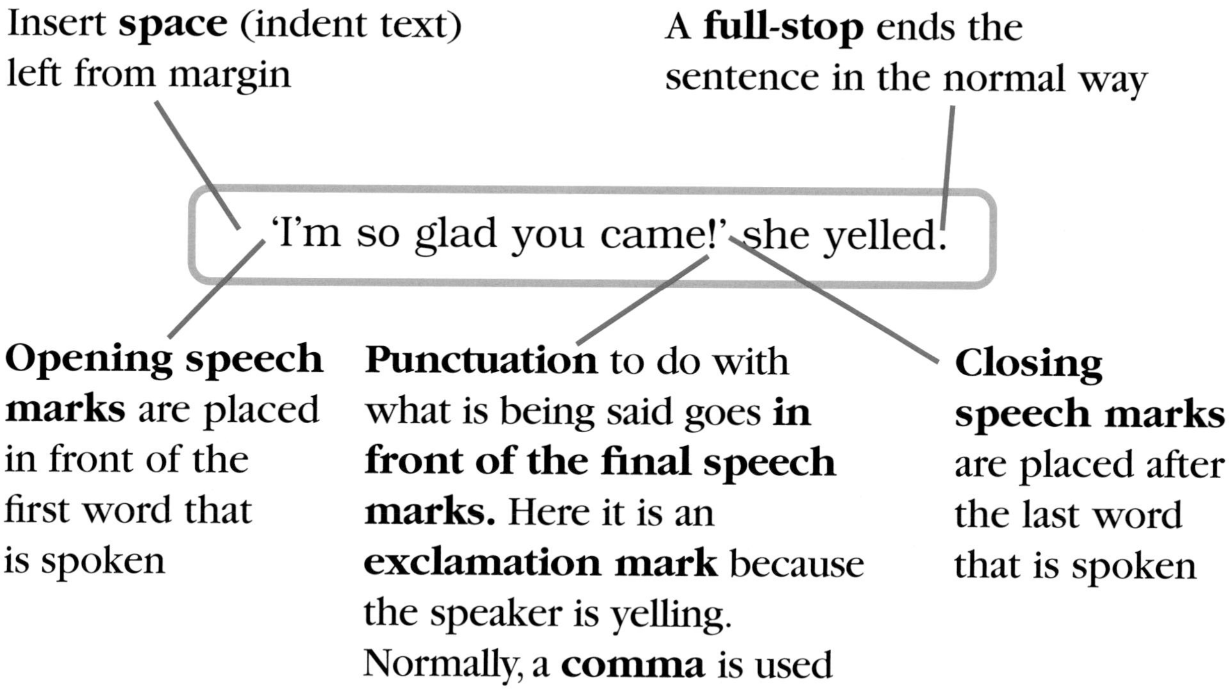

Insert **space** (indent text) left from margin

A **full-stop** ends the sentence in the normal way

'I'm so glad you came!' she yelled.

**Opening speech marks** are placed in front of the first word that is spoken

**Punctuation** to do with what is being said goes **in front of the final speech marks.** Here it is an **exclamation mark** because the speaker is yelling. Normally, a **comma** is used

**Closing speech marks** are placed after the last word that is spoken

S7 **7** Now look at this longer sentence from the story:

> 'Start warming up, Bhamra,' he said, giving my shoulder a squeeze. 'We're one-nil down.'

Notice:

- the **first sentence** of speech begins a **new paragraph**
- the **speech marks** come **before** and **after** each bit of speech
- the **comma** comes **before** 'he said'
- the **full-stop** comes **at the end of the first sentence**.

**a)** Discuss why the second sentence **isn't** a new paragraph.

**b)** Why isn't 'giving my shoulder a squeeze' in speech marks?

## Key Writing

**8** Imagine that Jess runs up to congratulate Jules after she finishes her goal celebration. Write down **what they say** to each other.

- Try to write three or four pieces of dialogue.
- Punctuate each piece of direct speech correctly.
- Start a new line for each new speaker's words.

For example, you could start like this:

> I ran up to Jules as she came back from the crowd.
> 'That was a great goal. I knew we could do it,'
> I shouted.

- Read a text about how to learn mountain biking skills
- Look at how instructions are written (S13d)
- Understand and use imperative verbs
- Explore time connectives
- Compose your own instruction text (Wr13)

**This text is taken from a book on how to learn mountain biking skills.**

## Advanced mountain biking techniques

The more you ride, the more you can improve your basic techniques so that your ride is faster, more comfortable and more controlled.

For advanced moves, such as the bunny-hop, develop the ability to transfer your weight on your bike, skilfully and smoothly. Move your weight backwards to reduce the weight on the front wheel. Move your weight forwards to lighten the weight on the rear wheel. To alter the amount the bike leans when you take a corner, transfer your weight from side to side.

Soon you will be able to make the bike do anything you want!

### Cornering at speed

To corner at speed, keep the leg and pedal on the outside of the turn in a downwards position. Keep the leg on the inside of the turn away from the pedal, ready to put it down in case you lean over too far.

Professional riders "drift", or skid, through corners, steering in the opposite direction to control a skid with both wheels sliding sideways, and applying the brakes. It's dramatic – but best left to the professionals!

## Jumps

25 Hitting a small lump in the trail can lift the bike in the air. Jumping is great, but because the bike is in the air, you're in more danger of hurting yourself. Start with small jumps; only progress to larger ones when you are confident. When you land, bend your arms and legs to reduce the impact of the bike as it lands.

## The bunny-hop

30 The bunny-hop allows you to lift both wheels clear of the ground at the same time. To look at it, you'd think it was impossible, but it's not! It is a useful move, 35 especially if you come across a log or a pothole on the trail.

Begin with a single-wheel bunny-hop. Ride at a walking pace; crouch down 40 and pull back on the handlebars as you push down on the pedals.

As you do this, the front wheel will lift off the 45 ground. Shift your weight forwards, pushing down on the handlebars. This will lift the back wheel off the ground as the front wheel 50 clears the obstacle. As you land, start to pedal.

For the double-wheel bunny-hop, stay out of the saddle and crouch down. Pull 55 on the handlebars and jump or spring the bike clear of the obstacle. Not easy, but practice makes perfect.

**technique** skilful way of doing something

**pothole** a hole in the road, so-called because it can look like a round pot

**obstacle** something (usually an object) in your way

## Key Reading

### Instruction texts

This is an **instruction** text. Its **purpose** is to tell someone clearly how to do something.

The main **features** of an instruction text are:

- It usually has a **clear design**, with a **step-by-step** approach often supported by **pictures** or **diagrams**, for example, photos that show the move.
- It has a **plain and simple** style, often using **connectives** of **time** or **sequence**, for example, 'When you land, bend your arms and legs to reduce the impact.' You need to be able to understand the instructions and follow them easily.
- It has **imperative** verbs. These are verbs that **tell** (or **command**) you to do something, for example, 'Pull on the handlebars.'

**1** **a)** What is this text instructing the reader about?

**b)** How many **different skills** does it deal with?

**2** Look at paragraph 6, beginning 'Hitting a small lump…' Find **two phrases** which describe doing something *at the same time* as something else. What is the **key time or sequence connective** that means 'at the same time'?

**3** There are many examples of **imperative (command) verbs** in this text. Find at least **three more** that come at the start of sentences.

### Grammar for reading

**Imperatives** are verbs. Normally these are verbs of physical action like 'run', 'shut', 'give', 'jump', etc. But they can also describe mental states, such as 'feel', 'think', or 'worry'.

## Purpose

The **purpose** of the text is to make the instructions **clear** and **easy to follow**. As you have seen, this is aided by the use of **imperatives**.

In *Advanced mountain biking techniques*, the writer uses imperatives to **tell** the beginner exactly what he or she must do. For example:

> *Move* your weight backwards to reduce the weight on the front wheel.

Putting 'move' at the front of the sentence makes it very powerful. Not all imperatives appear at the start of sentences, but many do.

This instruction is also a **command.** This is because the writer believes that this is the correct way to do it – no argument. As a learner, the reader **expects** to be told what to do.

**4** How does the effect **change** if you take the following instruction and add the phrases below to it?

R14

Look in your mirror before you reverse the car.

- You might like to…
- Why don't you…
- It might be a good idea to…

**5** Which one sounds the '**gentlest**' and least 'bossy'?

## Reading for meaning

The following questions focus on the **structure** and **content** of *Advanced mountain biking techniques*. However, they also refer to the **language** used by the writer. You should discuss the answers with a friend or in a group.

**6** The fact that *Advanced mountain biking techniques* is an instructional text is supported by the way the text is separated into four sections. What does the writer use to **highlight** the start of each new section?

**7** This is an active text about bike moves and moves with your body. In the first section, the writer uses a number of adverbs to describe how or where to move:

**adverb**

Move your weight backwards to reduce the weight on the front wheel. Move your weight forwards to lighten the weight on the rear wheel. To alter the amount the bike leans when you take a corner, transfer your weight from side to side.

In the first sentence quoted on page 203, the writer uses the adverb 'backwards' to describe the movement.

**a)** Find the adverb of movement in the **second sentence**.

**b)** Find the adverb of movement in the **third sentence**. (It goes with the verb 'transfer', which means 'to move from one place to another'.)

### Grammar for reading

An **adverb** describes **how** you do something. It goes with a **verb**. We often expect adverbs to end in *-ly*, for example, 'quietly', 'curiously'. However, there are many adverbs that don't end in *-ly*, such as 'backwards' and 'forwards'.

## Focus on: Instructions that are easy to follow

Clear instructions need imperative verbs, such as 'place', 'put' or 'keep'. However, instructions can also contain reasons *why* something should be done. The reason or effects described can be good and bad.

| Instruction | Reason or effect |
|---|---|
| Keep your eyes on the road… → | …or you may hit a pothole. (**BAD**) |
| → | …and you'll avoid the potholes. (**GOOD**) |

Note the use of the word 'or' to show what *might* happen.

Here is another example taken from the text:

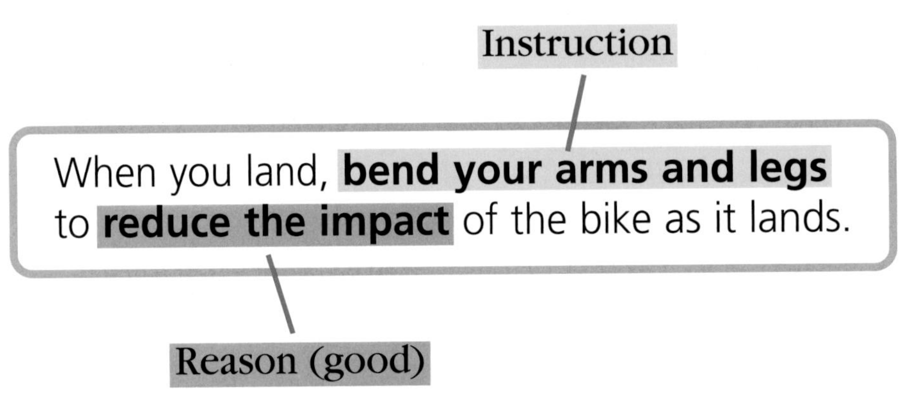

**8** Copy out the sentences below, adding the **effect** of an action. In this case, use the word '**or**' to show what might go wrong.

- Keep your eye on the pancake when you flip it in the air or…'
- Check that your dad's in a good mood when you ask for more pocket money or….'

## Key Writing

**10** You and your friends have been given the task of **organising** a **mini-tournament** for football or basketball for four local primary schools. The teams need to arrive at your school at 9 am on Saturday morning.

You need to send out a **set of instructions** to all the parents about:

- what their children need to wear
- what they need to bring
- when to arrive
- when the parents need to pick their children up.

**Discuss** the instructions you need to send, then **make a list** of those that you all agree on.

- Remember to start (where you can) with an **imperative verb**. For example, 'Arrive at…'
- Use **sequence words** if needed, such as 'Afterwards…'
- Include any other information. For example, 'The winners will each get a medal…'

# ④ Unit 9 Assignment: Sports reporter

## Assessment Focuses

- AF3 Organise and present whole texts effectively, sequencing and structuring information, ideas and events
- AF6 Write with technical accuracy of syntax and punctuation in phrases, clauses and sentences

**You:** are the reporter for a football magazine.

**Your task:** to write a profile of Thierry Henry for the magazine.

## Stage 1

You have already interviewed Thierry Henry and your notes are shown below. Unfortunately, they are not well organised.

Captained French under-18 team.
Born 17 August 1977 in Paris, France.
Signed for First Division Monaco under manager Arsene Wenger aged 13.
5 Scored most goals for France in 1998 World Cup.
Signed for Arsenal in Aug 1999. Renewed working relationship with Arsene Wenger.
Named PFA Players' Player of the Year in 2003 and 2004.
Married to model Nicole Merry. Met while filming TV ad for Renault.
10 Brought up in a poor suburb of Paris. Had a lot of support from family.
Signed for Juventus in Jan 1999.
Played first professional game for Monaco aged 17.
First game for France against South Africa in 1997.
Helped Arsenal to unbeaten run in 2003/2004 Premiership season.

## Stage 2

**Organise** the notes. Choose suitable sub-headings for each section of the profile from the following:

- Early life
- Signed by Arsenal
- France career
- Home life

## Stage 3

Turn the notes into a **profile**. Remember to add words to make **full sentences**, use the **past tense** and use **sub-headings** for each section.

For example, you could turn the following notes into the sentences below:

**Early life**

Thierry Henry
Born 1977
Lots of support from family

→

**Early life**

Thierry Henry was born in 1977 and grew up in a poor suburb of Paris. His family always supported him in his football.

### Challenge

You might want to add some **direct speech** to the profile. This means putting in some things that Thierry says. For example:

'My family were always supportive,' he told me.

Remember what you have learned about speech punctuation. (Check page 197 if you are not sure.)

William Collins' dream of knowledge for all began with the publication of his first book in 1819. A self-educated mill worker, he not only enriched millions of lives, but also founded a flourishing publishing house. Today, staying true to this spirit, Collins books are packed with inspiration, innovation and practical expertise. They place you at the centre of a world of possibility and give you exactly what you need to explore it.

Collins. Do more.

---

Published by Collins
An imprint of HarperCollins*Publishers*
77–85 Fulham Palace Road
Hammersmith
London
W6 8JB

Browse the complete Collins catalogue at
www.collinseducation.com



10 9 8 7 6 5 4 3 2 1

ISBN 0 00 719432 3

Mike Gould, Mary Green, John Mannion and Kim Richardson assert their moral rights to be identified as the authors of this work



British Library Cataloguing in Publication Data
A Catalogue record for this publication is available from the British Library

**Acknowledgements**

The following permissions to reproduce material are gratefully acknowledged:

Text: *The Shortest Horror Story Ever Written* from MORE HOROWITZ HORROR by Anthony Horowitz first published in the UK by Orchard Books in 2000, a division of The Watts Publishing Group Limited, 96 Leonard Street, London, EC2A 4XD, pp4-5; 'Big Fears' by John Rice reproduced with permission, pp11-12; extract from 'Ghosts: all in the mind' from BBC News at bbc.co.uk, pp19-20; extract from 'The Apples of the Hesperides' from THE ORCHARD BOOK OF GREEK MYTHS by Geraldine McCaughrean first published in the UK by Orchard Books in 1992, a division of The Watts Publishing Group Limited, 96 Leonard Street, London EC2A 4XD, pp28-29; extract from 'The Science of Superheroes' from BBC Science & Nature at bbc.co.uk/sn, p35-36; extract from 'Unidentified Flying Objects' from BBC Science & Nature at bbc.co.uk/sn, p50-51; extract from ONLY YOU CAN SAVE MANKIND by Terry Pratchett published by Doubleday. Used by permission of the Random House Group Limited, pp56-57; extract from *Alien Life (What's the Big Idea)* by Jack Challoner (Hodder Children's Books, 1998), p63-64; extract from *Holes* by Louis Sachar (Bloomsbury, 2000), p70-71; 'Should music take the rap for the increase in gun crime' by Matt Walton from BBC Collective at bbc.co.uk/collective, © BBC 2002, the BBC's consent must be obtained for all other uses (contact: Kate Reid, Legal and Business Affairs Manager 020 75571226), p77-78; 'The Trial of Derek Drew' from *Heard it in the Playground* by Allan Ahlberg (Viking, 1989) Copyright © Allan Ahlberg, 1989, reproduced with permission of Penguin Books Ltd., pp84-85; extract from *Two Weeks with the Queen: Play* by Mary Morris, based on the novel by Morris Gleitzman (Macmillan Children's Books, 1994), pp92-94; review of *Finding Nemo* from unreel.co.uk © Concept Publishing Ltd., pp106-107; extract from 'Snake bites' from the Australian Child and Youth Health Agency website at cyh.com, pp116-117; 'Bournemouth in the rain' © Bill Bryson. Extracted from NOTES FROM A SMALL ISLAND by Bill Bryson, published by Black Swan, a division of Transworld Publishers. All rights reserved, pp130-131; Wall's Carte D'Or advert reproduced with kind permission from Unilever ice cream and Frozen foods UK, p138; Blackpool Sealife Centre advert reproduced with permission, p139; extract from 'Is it time to stop worrying' by Lisa Markwell from *The Independent*, 1 May 2004, pp145-146; extract from 'Pen pal dangers' from *mizz*, 17 April 2002, pp152-153; extract from *Boy* by Roald Dahl (Penguin Books, 1992), p162-163; 'It was long ago' by Eleanor Farjeon from *Blackbird has Spoken* (Macmillan), pp169-170; extract from 'Ellen MacArthur: back on the high seas' from BBC News at bbc.co.uk, pp186-187; extract from *Bend it like Beckham* by Narinder Dhami (Hodder Children's Books, 2002), p192-193; extract from *Fantastic Sports: Mountain Biking* by Brant Richards (Aladdin Books, 1998), pp199-200.

Images: AA World Travel Library: p137; Advertising Archive: pp145, 146, 151; Alamy Ltd: pp77, 148; Alasdair Bright, NB Illustration: pp29, 31, 34, 85, 87, 89; Aquarius Collection: pp70, 71, 73, 75, 109, 110, 180, 193; Ardea: p120; BBC: p115; Bluegreen: p191; Buzz Pictures: p199; Coultard Institute: p181; Culture Archive: p184; Fogden Photographic Library: p116; Getty Images: pp12, 14, 18, 41, 50, 104, 152, 153, 200, 202; Idols Licensing and Publicity: pp78, 160; Jonatronix: pp25, 69; Lonely Planet Images: p119; Marco Schaaf, NB Illustration: pp57, 59; Mary Evans Picture Library: pp20, 24, 53, 00; Movie Store Collection Ltd: pp48, 107, 179, 192, 195; PA Photos: pp80, 124, 130, 131, 133, 187, 188, 207; Popperfoto: p162; Ronald Grant Archive: pp35, 36, 38, 40, 55, 66, 64; RSPCA Photolibrary: p117; Sarah Naylor, NB Illustration: pp4, 6, 8; Stephanie Strickland: pp170, 172; Sue Cunningham Photographic: pp123, 126

Whilst every effort has been made both to contact the copyright holders and to give exact credit lines, this has not proved possible in every case.

Printed and bound by

Printing Express Ltd. Hong Kong